"Whether it's a transition or a tragedy, we are all recovering from something, and we all need a little honesty and humor to make it through. That's exactly what Dana provides in *Bottled*. She's brutally honest about depression, alcoholism, triggers, pJourney through the messy and still recovering alcoholic, self-proclaimed control freak and 'zombie-mom.' You'll never look at carrot cake the same way again!"

Kasey Johnson, Author of *Mom Essentials, 7 Ways to Be a S.M.A.R.T.E.R. Mom,* and the blog SmarterMoms.com

---

"Dana discusses the serious topic of alcoholism, which affects millions of people, with humor and a whole lot of grace. Her recovery is inspiring and her journey is real, but her ability to laugh though the pain is what will heal the many who read this book. Moms will no doubt relate to it, but so will daughters, sisters, wives, and all women who need a friend to walk with them in early recovery. Dana is that friend."

Crystal Renaud, Author of *Dirty Girls Come Clean*

"*Bottled* is wildly entertaining, and provides a host of practical tips for moms going through the difficult stages of early sobriety. Dana reveals the very real and authentic struggle for moms in recovery, with humor and humility. A must-read for recovering moms, but also a wonderful book for any mom who may struggle with parenting small humans while attempting to stay sane."

Megan Peters, Author of the blog Crazybananas.com

Special Praise for *Bottled*

"An extremely touching journey from alcoholic mom to recovery hero, filled with brutal honesty but also a surprising amount of laughs. A must-read for anyone who can relate, knows someone who can, or just loves memoirs. Filled with helpful lists for the newly recovering and packed with laughs—I highly recommend!"

Stefanie Wilder-Taylor, Author of *Sippy Cups Are Not for Chardonnay* and the blog "Baby on Bored" at stefaniewildertaylor.com

---

"*Bottled* brilliantly illustrates the complexities of managing the roles of a wife, mother, and teacher who danced with addiction and, ultimately, emerged stronger for it. Bowman has an uncanny ability to bring out what is light and funny in even the darkest of times, with quirky How To lists at the end of each chapter."

Tonya Meeks, MA, LMFT, Certified Field Model Interventionist, Author of *Flying Standby,* and Creator of the workshop "Telling the Truth on Stage: Healing Trauma and Addiction through Performance"

"Full of vulnerability, courage, and grace. Bowman shares her story with wisdom and humor, and speaks to the beautiful messiness in us all: our struggles with perfectionism, fitting in, and all the feelings. A must-read for anyone who has struggled with addiction, but also a story for every mother out there. Sit back, pour yourself a cup of (freaking) tea and be ready to laugh, cry, and feel like you're not alone."

Ellie Schoenberger, Author of *Let Me Get This Straight,* Founder of Shining Strong, Inc. and The Bubble Hour podcast

---

"Without glossing over the gory details, Bowman tells her story with complete vulnerability, self-awareness, and humor. Her tips on surviving recovery and motherhood will help anyone navigating the sharper edges of life. She offers what so many addicts say they need: 'a Handbook for Life.' *Bottled* is funny, captivating, comforting, and full of hope."

May Wilkerson, Huffington Post Contributor and Former Senior Editor at Substance.com

---

"Whatever your particular struggle, do not miss this hilarious and redemptive memoir by Dana Bowman. *Bottled* will make you laugh out loud, nod your head in agreement, and maybe shed a few tears as Bowman shares a page-turning account of her journey through marriage, motherhood, and recovery."

Allison K. Flexer, Author of *Truth, Lies, and the Single Woman*

BOTTLED

BOTTLED

A Mom's Guide to Early Recovery

Dana Bowman

CENTRAL RECOVERY PRESS

LAS VEGAS

Central Recovery Press (CRP) is committed to publishing exceptional materials addressing addiction treatment, recovery, and behavioral healthcare topics, including original and quality books, audio/visual communications, and web-based new media. Through a diverse selection of titles, we seek to contribute a broad range of unique resources for professionals, recovering individuals and their families, and the general public.

For more information, visit www.centralrecoverypress.com.

Publisher: Central Recovery Press
            3321 N. Buffalo Drive
            Las Vegas, NV 89129

20 19 18 17 16 15   1 2 3 4 5

ISBN: 978-1-937612-97-9 (paper)
      978-1-937612-98-6 (e-book)

Photo of Dana Bowman by Erica Heline

Publisher's Note: This is a memoir, a work based on fact recorded to the best of the author's memory. Central Recovery Press books represent the experiences and opinions of their authors only. Every effort has been made to ensure that events, institutions, and statistics presented in our books as facts are accurate and up-to-date.

To protect their privacy, the names of some of the people and institutions in this book have been changed.

This book contains general information about addiction, addiction recovery, and related matters. The information is not medical advice and should not be treated as such. Central Recovery Press makes no representations or warranties in relation to the information in this book. If you have any specific questions about any medical matter discussed in this book, you should consult your doctor or other professional healthcare provider. This book is not an alternative to medical advice from your doctor or other professional healthcare provider.

Cover design by David Hardy
Interior design by Sara Streifel, Think Creative Design

To Christopher Scott

You are loved

Table of Contents

PART TWO: The During

PART THREE: The Now

Acknowledgments

To Central Recovery Press: Thank you for taking a chance on me. I hope to make you proud. And to Eliza, the coolest editor ever: Thank you for putting up with all my cat memes. You are simply the best.

To my sober sisters and brothers: You are my ever-present lifeboat. You kept saying, "It will get better," and yep, you were right. Thank you.

To the Booze-Free Brigade: I lift my La Croix to all of you. Thank you. You know how special you are.

To my church: I'm usually really good with words, but I can't really put into words just how much you mean to me. Thank you.

To my friends: All of the really good parts of this book are dedicated to you. I wrote them when you were watching my children.

To Jenni and Sherry: No, really. **Thank you** for loving me. And thank you for your evil sense of humor. We are family. And we really do put the "fun" in dysfunctional. I adore you guys.

To my mom: I'm really sorry about the bad words and the parts about sex. But I sure do love you. Thank you for your wisdom, your letters, and sweetness. You should write a book.

To my dad: You are my hero. Always have been. Always will be. I love you.

To my sweet husband: We make a good team. Thank you for not sending me back down to the minors. I love you so.

To Charlie and Henry: You are the best of the best, and I love you to the moon and back. Now, go to bed.

Thank you, sweet Jesus, for your love and all those times you said, "I'm here. Don't freak out." I'm sure that's in the Bible somewhere. You are my all in all.

And to all mommies, all of them, everywhere, who are sick and tired of being sick and tired. This is for you.

Introduction

> *"Self-love, my liege, is not so vile a sin*
> *As self-neglecting."*
>
> William Shakespeare

It took a wedding, two babies, and a funeral to help me understand I needed to get sober. How I survived parenting while in recovery is another story.

For me, the ugly cry involves a lot of snot and bravado. The snot is self-explanatory, but the bravado means I simply refuse to acknowledge the copious drips collecting around my nose. I won't wipe. I don't blink. I don't even call my bluff with a wet sniffle. Sitting in a squeaky pew at my brother's funeral, I have settled into the ugly cry. At this point there is so much beading of moisture I'm convinced I'll leak all over myself when I go up to give his eulogy. Meredith takes pity on me and hands me a Kleenex; it's the size of a postage stamp. I half-heartedly dab at one side of my nose, which only makes the snot spread, leaving a glistening snail trail over my once perfectly applied lip gloss.

At last I give in and collapse into my father's cotton handkerchief. I had asked him for it before the funeral, and he'd handed it to me without a word. I'd wanted it because I needed to hold on to something of his while I realized that his boy, and my darling brother, was gone.

My brother died because he drank too much.

I, also, drank too much. Here's the story of how I stopped, and how I keep *being* stopped every day, twenty-four hours at a time. I am in recovery, and I am a wife and a mother to two small children *all at the same time.* Having toddlers and not drinking seems quite a feat to some, and I completely understand. My drinking wasn't crazy when I was in my twenties, partying with friends. My addiction didn't bloom until my thirties when I was devastated by a broken heart. Instead it waited, patiently, until I had the one thing I always wanted: true love.

Now I had a husband, two babies, and a big fat addiction to alcohol.

Is parenting possible without wine? Even on a nut-ball, crazy toddler, Sharpie-marker-on-the-couch, Barney-on-repeat kind of day?

Yes. And, more importantly, even with the decorated couch, even with Barney, even when I can't find my keys, or my sanity, or a diaper, I found joy in sobriety. It's possible.

Not only is it possible, it is deserved.

PART ONE

The Before

"After the first glass, you see things as you wish they were.
After the second, you see things as they are not.
Finally, you see things as they really are, and that
is the most horrible thing in the world."

Oscar Wilde

CHAPTER 1

Birth with a Beer Chaser

My darling husband is leaning over me as I rest in the hospital bed with Charlie snoozing in my arms. Brian is smiling widely, but I am distracted because his pants seem to be . . . clinking? "My darling," he kisses me. "Here is your beer."

I don't like beer. An alcoholic saying she doesn't like beer is like a doctor saying, "I'm just not that much into stethoscopes. They're cumbersome." But beer's hops make my face itch, and whenever I drink it my nose twitches like a rabbit—and I sneeze a lot. I am willing to accept the irony that I really have an allergy to alcohol, as the Big Book says. But as I lie in my hospital bed, looking over at that brown bottle Brian had so proudly delivered to me from his cargo pants pockets, I thought, *Yes, please.* Then I looked down at the adorable scrunched-up face of Charlie, mere hours old, and thought, *No thank you. I'm scared. How did this happen?*

I know how it happened. Really, I do. I was there for the whole process. But right then, in that hospital bed, all I wanted was to be far away. Like maybe in Toledo, Ohio, at a bar. One where there are no kids or marriages or a second floor. My house has a second floor. It seems too much to deal with—two floors is a lot of responsibility. It is all so *grown-up*.

Back at the house with all those stairs, we have a chest of drawers that never opens or shuts properly. We banished it to the guest room on the second floor, of course. I'd bought it at a garage sale back when I was a single girl, and I wasn't getting rid of it because I'm too cheap. But it doesn't work. One drawer is wonky and has to be pulled in just a certain way if you want to access what's inside, and it won't shut without a lot of shimmying and sometimes a bit of terse language. I had, of course, allotted these drawers for my husband's underwear. Not that this makes sense. He needs underwear on a daily basis, and yet every day we deal with it, the slamming and the negotiation. The chest of drawers didn't fit in our lives.

It occurred to me that I should just move the underwear to a drawer that *works*. This idea was so practical that I knew it wouldn't see fruition for at least another year or so.

That drawer is exactly how I am feeling now, in that hospital bed, with my beloved Charlie in my arms. I don't fit. I really want to, and I know I am going to be so very needed. On a daily basis, I imagine. I hear babies are needy that way. But there's a lot of slamming and rather rough shoving going on in my head that sounds like this:

THIS IS THE MOST PRECIOUS MOMENT OF YOUR LIFE. JUST ENJOY IT. And then I breathe and try to eat some Jell-O, and Brian takes another picture of me eating Jell-O. *NO, NOW*

THIS IS THE MOST PRECIOUS MOMENT. YOUR HUSBAND IS SO ECSTATIC HE IS TAKING PICTURES OF HOSPITAL JELL-O. WOULD YOU PLEASE JUST ENJOY THIS?

And I smile and wobble the Jell-O for him, and think, *If he takes another picture, I am going to kill him. I am going to get up out of this bed, leaking all over the place, and hobble over there and smother him with my gigantic leaky body. I hate him.*

And finally, I shove myself in place with a solid, *WHAT IS WRONG WITH YOU? JUST FIT. MOTHERS ARE HAPPY WHEN THEY HAVE BABIES. WOULD YOU PLEASE, PLEASE JUST ENJOY THIS?*

So, you know, the beer kind of helped. I cracked it open and drank it down—nausea and all—while staring out of my large picture window. It was dusk, and I had a lovely view of a gray asphalt roof and a vent.

Charlie's birth had been difficult, which is sort of like saying World War II was tiresome. The entire pregnancy had been a challenge for me. When my husband and I married, we were what some would call "middle-aged." I was ancient at thirty-six, and my betrothed was nearly dead at thirty-seven. I was blessed with a husband who thought of children as something that must come in multipacks. He was from a large, loud family that had reunions all the time. They really liked each other, the Bowmans; therefore, they kept having more of themselves—all over the place.

One of our first dates was at yet another family reunion, where aunties, cousins, and nephews repeatedly informed me, "You know, he's never brought a *girl* to one of these things before!" Then they would look at me with such wonder and hope I was flummoxed. So I would blurt, "Well, here I am! And I'm

3

a girl!" and smile at the group of eighty or so Bowmans all eating barbecue and enjoying the heck out of each other.

By contrast, I came from a small family—small in every sense of the word. We are all short and don't hang out much. I never knew that family reunions were things that actually happened; they sounded like something goofy and wholesome, like something from The Waltons.

When babies were discussed after we married, I thought of it as some far off thing, like world peace—or the Royals winning the World Series. But, as sometimes happens in marriage, my husband had a completely different view. "We should have lots of kids! Lots of 'em! Like twelve!" I don't know how he came up with the number twelve. Perhaps because he has a thing for eggs—or the apostles. I don't know, but I do remember gently disagreeing with him by saying something like, "Good God, man, over my dead body."

Charlie decided to come into the world exactly on his due date. This is precisely how my son likes to operate. It was in writing, so he was there. Brian and I headed into the hospital at around 1:00 a.m. My water broke around midnight, and it felt like the baby was tap dancing on my nether regions about every thirty minutes.

I am actually in labor, I thought, as I peered out the window into the darkness surrounding our car. *Here I am, in labor.* I tested out the next sentence. *And after labor, there will be a baby.* Amazing how much I'd retained from those sex-ed classes. *And that baby will be ours. Like, we'll bring it home.* I felt very disenchanted with the whole idea. I kind of wanted to have the baby, yes. I was huge and tired and it felt like my vagina was permanently dislodged about three feet below where it should be. *But taking a baby and putting it in our house? Couldn't we just . . . check it out every once in a while and then return it?*

As usual, when things get overwhelming, I hummed listlessly and revisited my favorite monologue about my husband's inability to accelerate politely. "You're revving the engine!" I scolded. "It's not the Indianapolis 500, dear. It's just labor."

"I'm merging with traffic, dear," he countered grimly.

"You're merging like Mario Andretti," I offered. "And, this is a monologue. No heckling."

I'd had nine months to plan for this, to pray for it, and praise God for it. And here I was, feeling like I was in a movie, one with a funny heroine who was suckered into this whole pregnancy thing, with the hapless lover in tow, and a very short baby-birthing scene to follow. Once the baby was born, I'd be glistening with sweat and cuteness, and my sweet man would lean over to kiss me while I cuddled a non-slimy child. There would be a soundtrack from a John Hughes movie, and I would look into Charlie's eyes and be forever changed.

It didn't work out that way.

The actual birth with the dilation and the pushing was a tangled blur. I listened to that heart monitor slow down, and start up again, and then agonizingly slow down again. I rolled over like an accommodating whale that wanted to get a round of applause on this having-a-baby procedure. As the hours passed, Charlie just could not seem to keep up his heart rate.

One half of an epidural later—the local anesthetic had only taken on my left side, which I thought was normal—I was listening so hard to tiny erratic heartbeats that I felt my whole body pulsing with each faint beat. Charlie had no rhythm.

Then something changed in the room when the doctor quit being jovial and said, "We need to do a C. Right now." The room froze. I was hustled down a hall staring at the ceiling while whoever was pushing me ran the gurney into at least three walls and maybe a person or two. I couldn't find Brian. I thought the lights were terribly bright. This too seemed like a movie but not a happy one.

Later, I woozily told a nurse that I had a half-price epidural. "Could you please make sure my epidural is the sale price on the bill?"

I could tell you the whole story about the C-section and explain how traumatizing and invasive it feels. Because it *does* feel very, very wrong to have someone pulling around at your insides while you're awake for the show. Like that scene in *Jaws* where the geeky scientist cuts open a shark and starts throwing out all the innards from the stomach: a boot, some fish, a license plate, and general disgustingness. You know, after all that? I really felt for that shark.

The problem is that C-sections aren't all that new to modern medicine. I guess they've been around since, well, Caesar. And as much as I'd like to corner the sympathy market on how awful it was, I did just fine. Charlie did, too. We all got out of there alive, with innards smushed back in and intact. As my doctor, Dr. Boo, cheerfully put it, "Everything below your bellybutton is all jacked up"—thanks to the double whammy of long labor and then surgery. Dr. Boo was a great obstetrician, but he also lived up to his name. He freaked me out a bit. Still, the end result was a gorgeous little boy.

After Charlie's birth Dr. Boo announced, "It sure is a good thing for modern medicine! Without it you both would have been dead!" He grinned and mentioned the beer idea for breastfeeding. I stared at him blankly, and Brian patted my hand, realizing that this news might be a bit upsetting to a woman who just had her uterus placed *outside* of her body, where no right thinking uterus should be. I just nodded, yes, and then thought, *What did you say about beer?* Bedside manner was not my doctor's forte, so I did my usual upon hearing upsetting news: I pretended I didn't hear it and then filed it away to freak out about later. But I did hold on to that beer advice like it was a life preserver.

So I had a baby—despite myself. As I lay in that bed and contemplated the gloom descending outside, I couldn't help but wonder. *How in the world am I going to pull this off?* There was simply no way I could really *do* this whole mom business.

Once, when I was a freshman, the hottest fraternity at our college invited me to a large party. Their parties were epic. Their boys were of a bronze hue, so muscular and smart they were a walking Ralph Lauren ad. And here I was, being asked to mingle with them. The party was an invitation-only deal, and I still wonder how I managed to get the golden ticket for this one. I wasn't in a sorority, and I wore flannel a lot. I wrote poetry and played the flute. I wasn't a frat party kind of girl.

Of course I went. I put on a slightly hookerish Hawaiian get-up because the party had the creative theme of Beach Party at Fiji! I wore a lot of frosted lip gloss—so much that my long hair kept getting stuck in it as I tried to swish it around. As soon as I made it down to the dark and bass-thumping basement at the house, something in me clenched up with fear. I did not belong here. This was for stud football players and cheerleaders; these people were not my tribe nor did I want to be in theirs.

But I couldn't just *leave*. That would be pathetic. The only way to survive this kind of atmosphere was to have a big cup of the punch they were dolling out. The frat boys knew it; even the cheerleaders knew it. We were all a little bit scared. So I drank the Kool-Aid and danced the night away, eventually at ease and rather in love with every mook who attempted to make deep conversation while we shuffled along to Salt-N-Pepa. I fit right in. I even had fun. But part of me knew that without that red cup—there was simply no way.

Staring out my hospital room window, I blinked in surprise. I felt like that girl in the Hawaiian miniskirt and matching scrunchy. I had a new dance partner and only one beer to help me start the dance.

TOP TEN REASONS TO WRITE ABOUT SOMETHING YOU REALLY DON'T WANT TO

1. I have to redeem the fact that I used to wear neon colors and scrunchies.

2. Catharsis. This is one of those SAT words you learned in eleventh grade you can actually use later in life. Do not confuse it with the word "catheters." This can be a troubling experience on many levels.

3. It's always darkest before the dawn. What doesn't kill us makes us stronger. It's a blessing in disguise. Uh, a bird in the hand is worth two in the bush?

4. It's either this or take up croquet.

5. I owe it to my children and my husband. They are the binding, the pages, and all the ink. And perhaps I will make us millions.

6. I owe it to my friends and my community. They have been very patient with me.

7. Back to that millions thing: I am not kidding. Please tell people to buy this book.

8. If it is made into a movie, I want to be played by Sandra Bullock.

9. It's always a good experience to completely humble yourself. That's in the Bible somewhere.

10. I know you're out there, you tired mommies, who might need this book. I hope reading it helps you as much as it helped me to write it.

CHAPTER 2

I Never Danced on Tables

"Really, Dana. I do not understand why you cannot just HOLD HANDS." My parents are in bed; it's past midnight. My mother is glaring so hard I fear her glasses might explode. Explaining why I was late because my boyfriend's jeep got stuck in a field behind Metcalf South Shopping Center is not going well.

I am so humiliated. My response to shame and sorrow is to act like I am too sophisticated for this conversation, or even for parents. This makes my mother's glasses start throwing sparks. I slouch next to their door, willing the lecture to end, so I can somehow just droop away, undetected, perhaps until I am eighteen. I attempt to arrange my face into something between polite interest and sullen languor, twitching back and forth so much that I'm sure I end up looking rather constipated. My mother crosses her arms and waits, wanting a response, perhaps a promise, that my relationship with the total love of my life will become as platonic as a Nickelodeon show.

This is, of course, totally impossible. He is the total love of my life. Like, TOTALLY. It is the east and he is the sun, kind of love. Although when I did try to quote Shakespeare to the boy, he stared at me blankly and asked if that was from one of his mixed tapes of The Cure. My constipation increases as I try to find words to explain the gravitational tug of this everlasting and all-encompassing love that is my eternity. But all I can utter is, "He's just . . . and me . . . we are so . . . I can't." And, as is ever the case in every John Hughes movie, my parents *just do not understand.*

But then, I see it. On my father's face: just a whiff of a smirk. It travels across his mouth and settles for a second, but then he wipes it away and replaces it with a frown. And I wonder, *Is it possible he might understand the undertow of love a little more than I realized?* I know I saw it.

As time would tell, I would find out a lot more about how my dad and I are very similar.

It doesn't help that I show up covered in mud and boysenberries. Because, of course, we'd decided to park under a berry tree. Berry trees are romantic. Sitting under the stars, making out, slapping at mosquitos, his jeep slowly sinking into the muck—also romantic. But the entire backside of my white Bongo jeans was plastered with large red and purple splotches, the scarlet letter of snogging.

I'd seen *Sixteen Candles* and *Pretty in Pink.* I was well-versed in teenage longing—the type of love that feels like the Titanic but has absolutely no clue what to do with all its bigness. Teenagers in love are like OJ in the white suburban barreling down the highway. We are convinced we are in the right, but we're heading for disaster—just hopefully not jail.

And, as much as my relationship with this boy was already fraught with soap operatic drama, betrayal, tears, and several broken curfews and promises, I was convinced I could not live without him.

All of this was pretty normal for a sixteen year old. However, I also couldn't live without straight A's, first chair in band, a perfect pre-SAT score, a tiny body, and angst. A *lot* of angst. I had angst so hot-wired into my system that I even brushed my teeth with a sense of ennui.

One night, my mom found me out on the back porch pacing in circles. I was circling that porch like I wanted to drop and take a nap, like our dog Jake did for endless rotations before he finally flopped down. I was muttering and crying. My mom tried to interrupt my orbit. "What is wrong? Aren't you coming in for dinner?" I walked faster and heard her sigh.

"I can't right now. I just have to figure all this out," I waved at the air as if whatever was bothering me were circling my head, like angst-driven gnats. It was very possible it was just a geometry test the next day that had turned up the crazy in me to level red. Or maybe it was that I tried to kink my hair, and I now looked like the bride of Frankenstein and no amount of butterfly clips was going to fix it. I just remember that I had no idea how to stop walking in those circles, and that I felt like I might stop breathing at any moment.

"Meatloaf?" My mother lobbed her best weapon for compliance and comfort. Her meatloaf with the Heinz 57 glaze and a side of mashed potatoes could possibly fix all my problems. It really is so good I've joked that they should serve it at the

United Nations. But that night I shook my head. I had piled on so many expectations of myself that I was imploding and if I stopped walking in circles, I would fall away from the earth, untethered and alone.

My mom left, and I continued my revolutions until it got dark.

This behavior, of course, continued. I graduated with honors. I was the first in my class to land a teaching job. I bought a house in my twenties. I fell in love with men who were impossible so I could fix them. I just had to be the best. And when I wasn't, the world would tilt, and I would feel like someone was trying to scrape me off it, into the trash, where I belonged.

I know there's a God because during this whole mess, I never did a high dive into alcohol. I didn't drink until college, and even then I didn't drink excessively. Sure, there were many parties with me and the red Solo cups, but for the most part my drinking was average. There were no blackouts, no puking, no sinister men, and no dastardly behavior. Not once, not *once* did I dance on a tabletop. I'd always wanted to, but doing so would mean I'd had to be the best tabletop dancer ever, and I wasn't willing to throw my hat in the ring on that one. I regret that. If there was one thing I wish I had tackled back in my drinking days, it would have been a good bit of shimmying on a tabletop somewhere. I imagine I would have slipped and ended up doing the splits, a great finale but a difficult dismount. So it is a small miracle, I guess, that I never had enough booze in me to attempt it.

The other miracle here is that if I'd started drinking excessively in my twenties, I would probably be dead.

Rather strangely, my own addictive personality was exactly what kept me from binge drinking in the first place. There was simply no way I was going to be a drunk because that would mean failure, and that was not possible. I would sit at the Blue Moose with my boyfriend who one day, I was sure, would be my fiancée. (He did not quite see it that way.) I would tilt my head toward the people who were slurring, laughing too loudly, or leaning over too far. "Lush," I would whisper as I delicately sipped my martini. I never drank so much that if I was wearing heels I'd wobble. In my life, I didn't wobble.

Yet, always there, alcohol would patiently sit with me and say, "It's okay. I can wait."

TOP TEN WAYS TO DANCE
ON TABLES WITHOUT HUMILIATION

1. Travel to Europe by yourself. Don't think too much about it when you book the tickets. Try not to go into too much debt to take this trip. Just take it.

2. Run a race. Maybe even a long one that seems impossible at first. Don't think too much about it when you register for it. Just do it.

3. Have a four o'clock, Pandora 80s singathon in your living room every day. Don't think too much about how your children and animals scatter whenever this starts. Just hit that vibrato.

4. Sign up for a poetry reading. The kind where you are actually reading. *Aloud.* Don't think about it too much as you write your name on the sheet. Just go.

5. Start telling really bad jokes all the time to whoever will listen. This is amazingly effective at making you look like a fool but in a highly approachable way. Don't think about it too much when no one laughs. Just laugh a lot anyway.

6. Take a cooking class. Learn how to make croissants. Or chocolate mousse. Don't think too much about posting well-lit pictures of these on Pinterest. Just eat.

7. Stand up; just put one foot on the chair and then one on the table.

8. Look around you. Get your bearings.

9. Take a deep breath. Step up onto the table.

10. And then, dance.

CHAPTER 3

I Fall in Love, so All My Problems Are Solved

I saw him from across a crowded room. I really did *see* him standing there. Something was a small flutter in my stomach, and a voice in my head said, *See him? That's the man you're going to marry. Now get over there. You should at least go and say "hi."*

I did say hi. I even gave him a hug. He told me later he thought I was cute in my pigtails and baseball hat. He was wearing a T-shirt from NASA, and I inquired, of course, if he worked there. He just smiled and said it was from the gift shop. I was not deterred. Much later, after we'd been married quite some time, I told him that upon meeting him that night I put him down for a late afternoon wedding, a small, simple affair. His eyes got a little wide, as if to say, "I am married to a scary woman. But evidently, I had no choice."

Previously, dating had been a nightmare. I would wait grimly for whatever victim would be showing up at my doorstep, always a chilled glass of something strong in my hand. The fact that I could not go on a date sober was one of those red flags that waved at me from time to time. But the ritual remained: the date would start around 7:00 p.m. At around five o'clock, I would start pouring ice into a large tumbler, adding lime and then sloshing in a generous glug of Tanqueray. I would add a bit of tonic, stir, and then wait for that first drink. Condensation would form, and when my anxiety level seemed to be tipping me into a different stratosphere, I'd take a dainty sip. Waiting for a good twenty minutes, after I made the drink, to start slurping it, made it okay. Making sure it was a mixed drink, with separate parts and steps, made it okay. Buying only expensive gins and vodkas, never anything in a plastic bottle, or, God forbid, more than one bottle at a time, made it all okay. But the negotiation with drinking had begun.

And, in some ways, I guess it could have been all right. Many people can have a lovely cocktail or two before a suitor arrives. This makes total sense. There is nothing wrong with "taking the edge off."

Except, I was *all* edges. All the time. And I was anticipating the drink more than any other part of the night. With my track record, it might have been understandable. I'd become a Christian in my late twenties. This meant, I was sure, I would now find a hot, manly, completely normal Christian boy, and we would settle down and live the Christian dream of normalcy. Instead, during the eight years after I'd found Jesus, I found absolutely *no one else*. At times I had some pretty heated conversations with God about it. I felt a little shortchanged. As always, God listened, and then, in His absolute wisdom, set me up with the following guys:

1. Tom, who said he had Jesus but then also wanted to know if I would sleep with him after we got engaged. This was on the second date. And I met him at a bible study. *A bible study.*

2. Rick, who was so wimpy he asked me to step on a spider when we were on a picnic. I took the side of the spider.

3. Another Rick, who couldn't go out with me unless we prayed and fasted for forty days first.

4. Owen. Owen was actually great, but he had absolutely no desire to be dating me.

5. John, who wanted to find our song on the first date and then pounded the dashboard in rage when I informed him that this sort of thing happens on its own. "My ex told me not to do this!" he shouted. I was not sure if he meant the song thing or the date in general. I walked home from that one.

6. Jimmy, who was from Alabama and had an adorable accent. Jimmy was also a preacher and did tell me that if we married I would be expected to play the piano at his church. He was a great guy. I have no clue, to this day, how to play the piano. Good for Jimmy we broke up.

7. Speaking of accents, one guy broke into a British accent occasionally while we were on our date at Barnes and Noble. I had to ask, "Um, you seem to be speaking in a British accent?" His reply, "Oh yes, I like to do that." There was no further explanation. Also, there were no further dates.

My dating years, of which there were many, were full of men, but not a one was right. In fact, so many of them were so colossally *wrong* I wondered if I should start a business turning men into dateable material, and, for a small deposit and twenty monthly installments, enroll them. I'd call it "I've Got Issues!" I thought it would make a great profit.

Or, perhaps, it's just a teensy bit possible many of these guys were totally fine. In hindsight, the "It's not you, it's me" line make a lot more sense—except the first guy on the list. He was an asshole.

When I finally met Brian, I felt like I could breathe. He had no clue we were going to get married and live happily ever after, but I *knew.* And so, for the many months that we dated, I was blissfully happy. I felt like God had parted the clouds, leaned down, and boomed, "IT'S OKAY. YOU CAN RELAX NOW."

And so, I did. I relaxed so much that I survived the following activities:

- Planning a wedding within six months, and then, yes, *actually getting married.*

- Quitting my beloved teaching job where I had been working for over twelve years.

- Moving and then stuffing all my possessions, and his, into a tiny house that had one closet. *One.* Also, stuffing one large dog and one neurotic cat into this house.

- Dealing with a husband who worked long hours and traveled for weeks with his new job.

- Starting a new teaching gig at a school so large the principal never learned my name.

• Moving again after one year and starting yet
another job.

I think there's some psychological stress test somewhere that notes many of these events as significant. I am not sure pets in small places is included on the list, but it should be. Ask the pets.

I, however, seemed to be just fine. I had made my lists. I had it all planned. I prayed. I called my mom when I needed cooking advice. I was doing just dandy. My sister would call and ask, "How is it going? How's married life?"

"Fine! Just fine! It's awesome! This is great!" I used words like that all the time, and my inner English teacher cringed as I used my average word choice. But anything more specific was confusing to me. I was just *fine*.

At the same time, I would trudge through the front door of that tiny house, home from a rather horrible day teaching at a school where I never felt I fit in, drop my satchel, pat the very cooped up dog, and head straight for a glass of merlot. It had become the friend I could talk to at the end of the day, using more detailed adjectives. I deserved that wine, after all.

One afternoon after we moved in, I was unpacking and trying to shove too many shoes into that one closet, when I heard a strange slapping noise right outside our front porch. When I stepped out, I was greeted by roughly thirty naked fraternity boys, running up and through our yard (it was on a corner). When I say naked, I mean totally naked. Like, *pale* naked. Some were carrying beers. The beers hid some parts. Some boys said hello. Others just ran faster as I stared, slack-jawed. I hoped the slapping sound was the soles of their feet, but I'm not sure. This realization was so disturbing I texted Brian at work, "WHAT KIND OF PLACE IS THIS?" and he responded, "College town dear. Enjoy."

Well, I did. We lived two blocks from the main drag in this little college town, where bars and restaurants spawned with cheerful and funky glee. Manhattan, Kansas, was hipster before hipster was cool. There was a sleek and sophisticated hotel with a mahogany bar and low, gleaming lights. There were dives, places to dance on tables, and pool halls. There were greasy spoons with endless hot wings and huge hurricane drinks that were sweet and deadly. And, there were margaritas everywhere. Their sticky sourness beckoned to me like a siren, and so we walked down to this happy place three, four times a week. It was never hard to convince the husband. He loved the food and the football, and I used the football as an excuse. I loved the margaritas. I loved the fun. I felt like I was on a permanent honeymoon.

We drank and watched the game. We picnicked and brought a bottle of wine. We enjoyed an afternoon at the bookstore and then hit Annie Mae's for a quick cocktail. We met friends for pizza and beer. We got takeout Thai and paired it with a cold white wine. We drank and drank, and we got to know each other. Newlyweds in love.

At times things seemed a bit off. We fought at some bar surrounded by noise and too many co-eds. I walked home by myself, convinced I hated him. We fought on a Sunday morning on the way to church; I shrank from the possibility that Brian might not be the knight in shining armor I had imagined. I shut myself in my room, read a huge Cormac

McCarthy book in one day, trying to isolate and punish Brian at the same time. I played so many head games I could have enlisted for the CIA.

We had to adjust to being married, and it was very hard. This is common, and it's not the end of the world. But drinking just about made it the end of the world. I don't think anyone has ever had a booze-fueled argument with a loved one that ended in great compassion and understanding. Put a glass in my hand, and I am always right. This made things a bit stressful. I wonder if this behavior should have been included on that psychological stress test that rates life events: drinking heavily to smooth over all the rough edges. If you check yes, add ten million points.

One late night I was watching a movie, waiting for Brian to get home from work. The television blared light and sound across a darkened room. Norman, the dog, snored at my feet, and I kept checking the clock. I sighed. It seemed I was always waiting for Brian. He worked very long hours and had a long commute, but I wanted him home. He had swooped into my life, and now it seemed he spent so much of it swooping away. I felt sorry for myself and took another long drink of some very cheap wine.

Just down the street from our house there was a liquor store that had bargain wine in dusty boxes under the shelves. I would hunt amongst the boxes, priding myself on "trying something new," such as an obscure three-dollar bottle from some exotic location, like Burbank. I felt I'd hit the booze jackpot. It was like a Dollar General for drinkers. I was well stocked that night with my cheap wine, and as I sipped heavily on my budget merlot, I started to become a little angry.

Brian showed up much later. He was tethered to a job that was very new to him, and he was a perfectionist. This made for quite a few altercations between us about "late," and "time," and "love," and "why can't you . . . " kind of stuff. This night he was prepared. He brought me a Dairy Queen hot fudge sundae with peanuts and whipped cream—my favorite thing ever. I took it, walked out to the porch, and hurled it across the yard. The ice cream landed in a graceful white arc, painting our lawn. My husband looked on in disbelief, and I sobbed and stomped off to the bedroom. My dramatic exit was slightly dampened by the fact that the bedroom was only three steps away, and I had to do a weird little hip shimmy to get past the coffee table and the dog.

I had been drinking since four in the afternoon.

Marriage was the big "yes" I had been looking for my entire life. I had been gritting my teeth and waiting for it to happen for so long, and it seemed that once the possibility of it was finally here, I felt weightless with joy. I was loved. I was chosen. This was all I ever needed.

Until, of course, I found out that it wasn't.

TOP TEN WAYS TO SET YOURSELF UP FOR FAILURE IN THE LOVE DEPARTMENT

1. Assuming your cat is a good judge of character.

2. Dating someone who still has a Milli Vanilli tape way in the back of his stereo cabinet.

3. Dating someone who wants to high-five you after he makes out with you.

4. Dating someone, anyone, when you just really need to "work on yourself."

5. Not understanding the concept of "working on yourself." It's not a cliché. It's not something therapists say to make more money. It's for real. It's the interception play that ends the game. Until next season.

6. Figuring your partner will change. If this is how you operate, just get some cats and plants and get bitter now.

7. Regarding your significant other as you would oxygen. This puts a lot of pressure on the significant other, and on oxygen, to complete you.

8. Dating someone who quotes *Jerry Maguire* to you with no sense of irony. Especially the "Show me the money!" part.

9. Allowing yourself to love *Jerry Maguire,* just a little bit, even though it has that crazy guy in it, but insisting that there is no way you can have romance, love, and mushy stuff, too. You can. You're worth it.

10. Not knowing what you're worth. Always know your worth. If you don't, someone else will assign it to you and will want you to change.

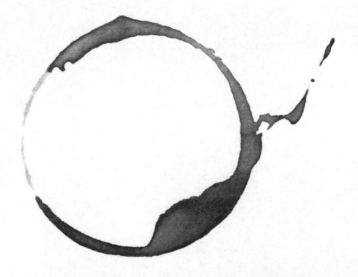

CHAPTER 4

All My Problems Are Not Solved

"Are you going to leave him? I mean it. *Should* you?" This is my pastor, staring at me with piercing blue eyes, asking me if I should leave my husband. And all I can do is sit there, mute and tear-streaked. For once in my life, I have absolutely nothing to say.

The first year of marriage is frosted with happy, romantic memories. Long walks on the beach. A lot of deep talks by a roaring fire. Meaningful looks. Romantic passion. All of it. At least, this was what I imagined it would be, during those *long* thirty-six years that I waited for my Prince Valiant.

There were a few problems here. First of all, the nearest beach was at a brown lake strewn with beer cans. We didn't have a fireplace. We did have a lot of candles, but the cat kept singeing his whiskers on all the ambiance. There were a lot of meaningful looks, at least from me, but I'm not sure Brian was really tracking any of those, so there was angry ambiance. And yes, sex did occur, as expected. We aimed for passion, but really, bedroom antics were not so much the cinematic kind. They were more like the "I'm trying to figure all this out, but I'm a little lost here. I know tab A fits into slot B and all, but I wish I had some clearer instructions" kind.

Here's what really happens when two people get married: all hell breaks loose.

I mean it. In faith, we stepped up to the plate together, fully committed to God's blessing and forming a covenant, like, in the eyes of God and the government, and my dad, and all that. This is big stuff. And so, from there on, it's pretty much a crapshoot. The scientists will tell you it's entropy. Theologians will say Satan. If I had asked my dad back then, he would have said "booze," which really is just a combination of both ideas.

When we first moved into our little love nest with the one closet, I felt so fluffed up with joy and marital bliss I might have taken flight. These feelings lasted as long as it took for me to understand what unpacking meant. The tiny bungalow we had rented was the size of one of those lovely showrooms at IKEA. Cute with a lot of great Scandinavian trinkets—no space. And in it, I needed to fit a stadium-sized share of boxes, packed full of pictures, candles, dog beds, and dishes— all from home. As I unwrapped each piece it would exhale homesickness into the air, like decor spores. Also, there was just too much of it. I had three coffee makers, no drawers, six closet organizers, and *one closet*. For weeks I unpacked, cried, and found myself going mad among piles of boxes as high as my head, weaving around them like a frustrated mouse stuck in a frustrating maze of nostalgia.

What I had not bargained for, among all these feelings and such, was that my sweet husband's behavior did not match up with what I'd had all planned out for him. I imagined Brian would be a hybrid of Dr. Phil, Ryan Gosling, and Jesus.

Here is how it played out in my mind: I'd be upset, perhaps a little sad and missing my home, when my sweet hubby would arrive home with flowers and wine (of course) to talk, soothe, and listen. Instead? My sweet hubby would not get home often until late, sometimes with flowers, sometimes not, and for some reason he was totally unable to read my mind.

I started teaching at the local high school about four weeks after we were married. Teaching had always been my passion and my joy, but my year at this school beat the joy right out of me. Classes were overcrowded. The faculty was in turmoil—gossip and grumbling was the norm in the faculty room. The building had mold problems, and I got dreadfully sick. All of this nearly broke my little Type A heart. Teaching was my *thing*. I was good at it and had plaques to prove it: Teacher of Excellence! Risk Taker Award! But none of these mattered to my new colleagues, and I couldn't put them on the walls anyhow. The walls were made of cold, hard cement that always seemed slightly moist with despair.

So, at the end of a day at school where the police had come, yet again, for locker searches—the dogs so loaded down with loot the officers would high-five each other in the halls—I would come home, exhausted, to our overstuffed house. The cat had peed in the corner again. He hadn't liked moving any more than I had, it seemed. My dog was joyous to see me; so joyous, in fact, he had chewed up the front curtains on the door for a better view. I could hardly blame him; with no fence in the backyard, he was cooped up all day in our dollhouse and was just about ready to lose his dog mind.

But once I trudged through the front door, taking the three steps into the kitchen, and cracked open a beer, something in me would crack open, too. I would feel better. A lot better. Because really, I deserved a beer. Police dogs were involved. My life seemed to be falling on top of me. A beer or two were completely understandable.

I hated my job. Which made me wonder—if being a teacher was all I had ever wanted in life, was all I was about, and now it wasn't, then who was I? And if being back home had been so much more comfortable and happy, with a great job and faculty who actually knew my name and frequently gave me awards lauding my fabulousness, was it just a teensy bit possible I had made a mistake?

What was more important? The job? Or the husband?

And if I was thinking about all this stuff, did it mean, maybe, just maybe, that I should not have gotten married at all? Should I have stayed put and invested all that wedding money in a good therapist?

What if I didn't really love him? And what if my cat continued to pee in this house? Would we ever get the deposit back?

I drank more beer. It made me worry less about the deposit.

Brian came home. There's this scene in *Apollo 13* where all the engineers are faced with the dire emergency of getting the spacecraft safely home, and the only things they have to work with are some paperclips, shiny tubing, and a few sticks of gum. I was pretty sure Brian's job was like that on a daily basis. Only his face that night told me that the astronauts at his job didn't make it that day.

I opened another beer and handed it to him. Then I said, "Today at school they found bats in the doorway to my class. I have bats in my classroom."

"Huh," Brian said.

I continued, "Yep. Bats. Crazed flying attack bats. Mice with wings flinging themselves at the children. It's appropriate, really. Fitting. That building is about as cavernous and pleasant as Vlad's castle. The bats simply add to the ambiance."

That was Brian's cue. I waited for him to respond something like this:

"I am so sorry honey. That must be really hard. I know you miss your home and your friends. I realize, too, that today you came to the startling realization that you are questioning everything about your teaching future and your new gig as a wife and all. And yes, you had to clean up cat pee on top of it all? It's simply awful. I have *ripped you away* from your home and family and put you in a town where the schools are not bat free. And, to top it all off, we probably won't get back our deposit. We are doomed."

Instead, he said, "Well, at least they eat the mosquitos."

Did I mention my husband is an engineer? Always practical. I wanted to kill him.

So, we fought. And we made up. I tried to keep the honeymoon going to give me something to celebrate after the gloomy job I faced. But I got increasingly angry at Brian's late nights and workaholic tendencies. And he got increasingly tired of my bickering and nagging. And so we fought some more.

We really did love each other. But we were so broken.

Brian had lost his mother to cancer in his early thirties. He had a lot of pain left from that, which he channeled directly into anger. Brian would lose it over forgetting to call someone back or misplacing a wrench in the backyard, so I would go in the bedroom and shut the door. While lying on the floor, I would cry and pray, completely lost as how to deal with a husband who was so loud and fearsome at times. When the storm would end, I had arsenal. My husband was just terrible. He yelled. He shook the windows of the house with his stomping. He was a tyrant, and it was simply inexcusable. True, the house was the kind that when you sneezed it leaned over a bit, but that wasn't important.

We started therapy with our church pastor. This is always a great option, and it helped me realize something that's essential for newlyweds to grasp: We are stuck with each other forever.

Forever is a long time. Especially when your husband uploads Quicken on your ancient laptop at 1:00 a.m., and it doesn't go well because it's technology, so he becomes unhinged. The computer stood up to the yelling with stubborn pride. I, however, found myself filled with rage, and I screamed right back at him. I knew I couldn't change it. I couldn't go out there and soothe or yell or show up naked and insist on sex to change it. He was mad at our computer, and himself, and there wasn't a thing I could do to help.

Later, when I told him about my frustration with all this, he sighed and said, "I am really sorry. I am working on it. And I think the showing up naked thing is an excellent idea. Let's try it."

The thing was, all of his anger was directed at himself. Not a bit of it was directed toward me. Not the yelling, the message, or any of it. He simply loathed himself. And then, when he found that darkness welling up inside of him, he loathed himself even more and would collapse under the pressure of needing to be perfect, a big implosion of impossible expectations. And all the while I watched with simmering resentment. I had a loud and easily identifiable reason for my misery, living right here next to me in our Habitrail. The problem was easy to spot: it was the loud, yelling one over there! In the other room! Freaking out about something he had done wrong. And here I was, the quiet one, praying. Faultless. Burdened. Very spiritual, too.

Therapy with our pastor did help; he was brilliant and caring and worked hard with us to find a solution to the outbreaks of anger and to all the communication problems. He had quite a job ahead of him. Brian was a mess. There was tons of work to do—on him. I was just the long-suffering wife.

"Do you think you should leave him?" My pastor asked me. I stared at him, then at Brian, and gulped. Why was this on me? Why couldn't we establish that this was intolerable, and Brian had to stop it right now? I mean I had done my time. I had waited and waited and then married a man who loved Jesus as much as I did. So, therefore, didn't that mean somehow everything from here should be a bit easier? Singlehood in my late thirties had been about as fun as a long walk through Chuck E. Cheese's with someone else's kid; a lot of squealing and noise, and a couple of balloons—a lot of suffering and counting the clock. I deserved a happy marriage after all *that*.

Brian stared down at his hands. I looked from him to my pastor, and back again. "No . . ." I said. My voice was so small it sounded like the air leaking from a tire. "I am not going to leave him. But . . . I just don't know how to live like this." Brian turned to me, his face full of pain, as if to say, "I have always lived like this. I don't know how *not* to live like this."

And then I realized it. This is how I dealt with the world: smooth it all over, like frosting on a cake, and insist on happiness and sprinkles for all. Be very quiet and nice and don't ever, ever upset anyone. Walk very softly and simmer on low, like a crockpot of resentment.

Brian dealt with things differently. Blow up to let off steam, stomp around, and then proceed. Be loud. Upset people. Get over it.

How charming. I had married the complete opposite of myself. I am sure this has never happened before in the history of marriages.

I would like to clarify that Brian's anger was totally inappropriate; it was loud and it was a bully. But it was just that—anger. Not violence, physical or mental harm, or threats. Brian's anger was so self-directed I am surprised he survived it. But since I was in the vicinity and was terrified of things going wrong, people being upset, and anyone ever feeling anything but happy, his anger terrified me. It should have terrified him, but he was used to it by now as a rather effective outlet for his pain. It sure did give me a lot of excuses to start drinking more.

His fault. *All* his fault. Drink up.

TOP TEN WAYS TO AVOID AN EARLY MARRIAGE ON THE ROCKS

1. Invest the time and commitment in counseling. Take as much time as you would arguing and simmering and divide it by at least five. That should equal about the amount of time you will spend in a counselor's office talking. And even if the counselor is lousy, it's at least one hour out of the week or month you will spend not shouting.

2. Understand that marriage is about the hardest thing you will ever do and you have to do it with another person. It's a group project. If you hated those in school, you might have some trouble here. Go back to the start of this list.

3. Give your counselor at least three visits before you decide that it's not working and not worth the money, time, long car trip in silence afterward, and so forth. Then go for *three more visits.* If it still isn't the right fit, *then* you can switch to another counselor. *Do not, under any circumstances, attempt marriage alone.*

4. Waiting for your spouse to change because it's all his or her fault is like hoping the lines will be shorter the next time you get your driver's license. Just work on yourself.

5. And maybe, just maybe, it's not all your spouse's fault. Work on yourself.

6. Also this: work on yourself.

7. Keep working. Get rid of the crockpot of resentment. Fill it up instead with the soup of self-love. Cheesy, but true.

8. Don't add mind-altering substances or alcohol to resentment and anger. It only makes the gnat that is buzzing around your ears the size of a stealth bomber. When you find yourself getting out the heavy artillery because your husband bought whole instead of 2 percent milk, you might want to lay off the sauce.

9. Try not to worry about the deposit. Some problems, like neurotic cats with angry bladders, are unavoidable. Also, do not try to train a cat. Do not try to train a spouse. Which leads me to:

10. Work on yourself.

CHAPTER 5

We Go to Paris and Fight the Whole Time

I am standing outside of Notre Dame Cathedral. The air is cool and a light gray mist graces my cheeks. The gothic church's stone and stained glass soars above me in Parisian extravagance, and all I can think is that I need to find a bathroom. And, if my husband ever comes out of that cathedral, I am going to kill him. *Right here,* I think, *in front of all these cool Parisians.*

I am pregnant. And I don't really want to be pregnant. I am scared and stuck and, of course, my husband and I took a romantic vacation to Paris.

Paris does not have any bathrooms. There is one in our hotel room, but trust me, there are no other bathrooms in the entire city. I should know. My husband ambles about and takes pictures, looking at plaques below statues (Who does that?) and commenting on things like *history* and *culture*, while I nervously eye some sophisticated Parisian bushes that might offer some cover for my next potty break.

I was three months pregnant. We were in Paris, and I really wished I were home on our very American couch.

Here's how a Parisian vacation with your husband of three years should look: making out by the Seine, enjoying some crepes, and then taking twelve million obligatory pictures by the Eiffel Tower.

Here's how our Parisian vacation played out: freezing rain, grim determination, and a lot of crepes. I ate more crepes than a French teenager after football practice. There was a small kiosk right by the hotel that made them about the size of a car tire and slathered them with Nutella. Crepes upon crepes.

And, I drank absolutely no wine. No cognac, either. We didn't seek out the dark Parisian bars with sullen bartenders and a lot of gleaming bottles. No wine tastings. No wine cellars. There was no wine on my Paris vacation. This was just wrong and terrible. A tourist should be allowed to drink herself through her European vacation. It's the American Way! Europeans drink wine over here at lunchtime, and it's okay, *d'accord?* (Translation: "d'accord" means Paris is to drinking as the Kardashians are to eyelash extensions.)

I have had the pleasure of visiting Paris a few times. By "a few" I mean three, and one of those visits just involved the Paris airport, but still—it counts. My first *real* trip to Paris was on my own, and it was simply magical. In the great words of Mariah Carey, "I had a vision" of Paris, and it was all that Paris gave to me. My first morning in that glorious city, I walked out of my hotel room and looked to the right, and there, framed perfectly by the narrow road and white hotels, was the Eiffel Tower. It brought me to tears. I quickly hid behind large sunglasses and a disinterested slouch; I was going to blend in here, and sniffling and pointing at the Eiffel Tower was no way to get on my Parisian cool.

My first night in Paris I went hunting for what I envisioned the apex of Parisian experiences: cognac and no filter cigarettes— so strong the packaging doesn't even offer a warning, just a hotline for the nearest cardiologist.

I found a bar, composed myself into what I hoped looked like a tired model just going in for a nightcap before heading home to her Parisian apartment, Parisian cat, and tousled Parisian bed. I slouch-walked in, sidled up to a stool, managed to order "un cognac, s'il vous plait" with so much disaffection the bartender might have thought I was slipping into a coma at any moment. And I drank up.

It was *awesome.*

I have never forgotten that cognac, that stool, the bartender's dirty towel, or the loud couple to my right talking in their nasal snarl. It was like being on a movie set, and it was all I had ever wanted. Me, my cognac, and Paris. We were in love. The cognac and me were pretty much inseparable for the rest of the trip.

The fact that I programmed wine and cognac on repeat during the trip is understandable. I was terrified. I wanted so badly not to be pegged as a tourist. But I knew I was in a city where I barely knew the language, and I was terrible at reading maps, so at some point my cover would be blown. I walked around feeling like I was being watched and judged by the Cool Parisian Task Force, agonizing over my accent, my scarves, and my lipstick. I received the best compliment of my life when I ventured into a patisserie and managed to order an entire box of macaroons—cookies that are the color of Easter eggs—without breaking my cover. It wasn't until I accepted my change that I blew it and thanked her in English. She widened her eyes in surprise, and I realized I had fooled her! Maybe, *I fit here*!

Paris was so daunting. The Grand Prix of fitting in. If I could do it here, I could fit anywhere.

And that was so very important.

Now I am here in Paris, some four years later, and nothing fits. Not my jeans. Not my jackets. Not my communication skills with my husband. I can't slide into a warm cognac to help ease all these jangled nerves and anxious edges. I am a spectacular mess of not-fitting. My husband has not-fitting down to a cheerful science, mainly because he insists on wearing white tennis shoes for the duration, which is clearly against Parisian law. I am unable to care about the Louvre, St. Chapelle, or the Seine. I am very interested in crepes and places where I can sit. We head over to another monument, and my interest extends only to the benches surrounding it. I do love those crepes and devour numerous ones before lunch with a low moaning sound that makes Brian eye me uneasily.

Yes, it's possible I would have chosen the crepes over my husband. Along with the startling realization that bathrooms are too pedestrian for the French, I came to understand that traveling with my husband is rather difficult. He is an engineer and has a plan for everything. When Christmas comes, and we receive a large electronic gadget of some type, he is gleefully in that box, sniffing around for the instructions. He unfurls them with great pleasure and will proceed to read them with a pile of unopened presents still sitting before him. I am not sure he is human.

I am of the firm conviction that instructions are a waste of time. I "throw things together." I "rig stuff." I don't "follow the straight and narrow," because "that's for pansies." Why? I don't know. Straight lines are boring. In the case of this trip, some basic instructions like, "Plan ahead just a bit" would have helped. I didn't plan anything for Paris, down to bringing the wrong type of clothes to wear in the frigid weather. When my husband gently inquired about all this, I responded with remarks like, "Details are annoying" and "Leave me alone." As much as I value planning and organization, for some reason, I decided we were on vacation so I adopted the theme of, "Hey, let's just wait and see!" This all stemmed from a deeper theme of "I am absolutely terrified of this trip for some reason!" Incidentally, quotation marks gloss over a lot of fault lines in my personality. In hindsight, there should have been a bit more planning on both our parts, but I had insisted I would do it all, and then I didn't.

Before we left, it would have been good to look over the materials list for our trip:

- 1 Newly pregnant wife so tired she can master napping while standing. *Oui!*

- 1 Overenthusiastic husband who is fired up about the availability of ESPN in France. *Oui!*

- 2 Completely differing views of how this vacation should proceed. *Oui!*

We were doomed.

We were also doomed, of course, because I was scared about being pregnant. Yes, I was also scared that Brian would wear K-State everything and mangle his French—those fears were pretty much realized at the Paris airport. I was scared we would get lost a lot, and we did. And I was scared that I would somehow get separated from Brian, and there wouldn't be any crepe makers *or* a bathroom for miles around. This, thankfully, did not occur. But mainly I was *deeply* freaked out about having a little one growing inside me. I was so not ready for this whole baby thing. And this scratched at me because I wanted and needed to fit in. Fitting in would be: going to Paris, taking a lot of pictures of "le baby on board," and glowing about it the whole time.

Instead, my anxiety levels were at code red, which means disaster was set to strike at any moment. Feeling ill at ease and abnormal were actually *normal* for me. This trip packed all those uneasy feelings, along with a tiny baby and an uncomfortable bladder, into my tired body. I was surprised I was able to buckle my seatbelt over this entire bloated malfunction on the plane. But of course I did, because we were probably going to crash and die, most likely while we were over the ocean. The latest technology was kind enough to show me exactly how *much* of this trip was over the water through a handy-dandy massive screen detailing our trip on the cabin wall right in front of us. Of course Brian found this to be helpful and interesting. I just stared at the expanse of blue on the screen and nervously looked around for extra flotation devices. I would be floating for two.

Today I know that anxiety is a real ailment, not some floating feeling that surfaces from time to time, but an actual, diagnosable problem. Anxiety can be dealt with and treated. It didn't have to be scooted around in my brain as something silly. Clearly, my issues with anxiety were not going to go away, but so far, I had only dealt with them in the most logical way I knew how: have a glass or two of wine and voila! I am okay. Edges are muted. Fears are eased. Or, at least they are all spread out, like melted butter on toast.

At that point I had six more months of no more smoothing the sharpness and folding the corners down. I had to deal. And I had to be happy about it because it's a *baby* after all, not a prison sentence. How I hated myself for not wondering about the magic that was going on in my nether regions. After three months in, all I could feel was nauseous, and looking at a glass of juice made me want to pee. I didn't feel maternal or glowing. Just bloated. And very angry with myself.

Self-directed anger tends not to sit well with me, so I argued with the nearest target instead: my rather clueless and thrilled-about-all-that-water-below-us husband in the seat to my right. And the fights continued, all through the trip.

"Look, there's a museum over there about World War II. Cool!"

"I need to pee."

"You do? You just did over at the museum about all the dead people under the city. Again?"

"I don't care about World War II. I just need to sit. My hips are widening as we walk. I feel like I'm giving birth right here, for Pete's sake."

He eyed me and my hips and looked very unruffled.

"Dear, it's impossible to go into labor this early in the pregnancy. Unless, of course, there are complications or something." As the words left his mouth, I saw it: that slightly befuddled, blank expression he makes when he realizes his inner engineer just said something very cold and clinical, which is about to clash with the overly emotional vat of weeping that is his wife.

"How *could* you say that to *me*? I just can't *believe* you would even say such a thing."

"I'm *sorry*. I just meant that—"

We had now become the battle of the loud talkers. Very Parisian people walked past us and smiled. They were right at home with irritated loud talkers.

"You do not care at all about my comfort. I am miserable, and all you care about is if we have enough museums stuffed in us by the end of the day. *I hate you.*"

"What? You hate me? Really? No. Listen, we're on vacation." He gestured around helplessly, to help remind me that we were in a different time zone and all. I sniffled in the background. "I just . . . well it seems to me you're being just a bit—"

"*Don't you dare say it!*"

He said it. As the word "over-dramatic" left his mouth, I already contemplated how much it would cost to buy a separate plane ticket home and a separate house to live in when I got there. Brian, who at this point had realized this trip didn't have "fun-filled vacation" written all over it, fumed off in disgust to look at something about Hitler.

I fumed off to find some place to sit, in the sullen hope that somewhere close by I'd find a gleaming, tacky McDonalds with a large booth, and, of course, an even larger bathroom.

TOP TEN WAYS TO TRAVEL LIGHT AND STAY SOBER WHILE DOING SO

1. Sobriety is not a prison cell. Repeat that one million times.

2. Release all expectations. Release them to your Higher Power, your God, or just scream them into a pillow, if need be. Traveling can be wonderful. Expectations of wonderfulness are not.

3. Plan ahead. Don't wing it. Don't fly by the seat of anything. Know your triggers and plan ahead.

4. Avoid airport bars. They are triggery and full of people who are, can you believe it, drinking. The gall. Instead, get a Cinnabon. They have fewer calories than four gin and tonics. And ultimately, they're less embarrassing.

5. Plan also for failure. You will get lost. You will have a meltdown at the Eiffel Tower because the line is four kilometers long. You will eat snails. It will not go as planned. It is times like these that the Serenity Prayer is really handy.

6. Sober travel sometimes has to be, well, more expensive. Sometimes, recovery has to trump searching for a cheaper hotel or meal. Rest is crucial. Food is crucial. Not getting angry because your room is the size of a stamp is crucial.

7. However, if the only place you can find to grab a bite is a pub with gigantic, sloshy vats of beer, and everyone in there seems happy and sloshy too, and you start to feel a little bit left out, then pack a lot of food that's really bad for you, like about sixteen million Reese's Peanut Butter Cups. Get mega packs. Also, keep your phone handy with meaningless games like Candy Birds or Angry Farm or whatever. There will be times of tired waiting and thinking. Stop thinking and numb out with technology and sugar. They're good for you!

8. Don't pack it *all* in. Plan for down time, for time to sit and watch the world. Don't go to every museum in Paris, just so you can say you did. Sit by some water and feed some sobriety ducks.

9. Above all else, don't look at the screen with the plane and the blue stuff. Watch a lot of movies and, if need be, scoot way down in your seat and take a much-needed nap.

10. It is my gentle suggestion not to travel while pregnant and a nervous wreck. In the same vein, don't travel while newly sober. Everything then is super hard, loud, and jangly, and you sort of need to hunker down and take care of your soul and yourself. Travel a lot *later*, so you can celebrate that you had the baby and got sober and are now totally on top of the world. Then, go see it!

CHAPTER 6

Zombie Mom

My son Charlie and I are on a walk. He is perched up in his stroller, peering out at the world like the captain at the prow of his ship. He points and directs our path. Fall leaves swirl in red clouds at our feet. The air has the tang and slanted sun of a late October dusk. We are a portrait. And I am miserable.

First of all, my head hurts. It hurts in a pounding, angry way, as if the entire top of my skull had decided to stomp on me every time I move. Actually, the stomping occurs whether I move or not. Thus, the walk. I couldn't stand to stay in the house as the dusk approached and enveloped the rooms with its shadows. I had to get out.

Secondly, my hands shake. No, this is not the telltale sign of alcohol detoxification. I wouldn't see that symptom for another two years. My hands are shaking because my body is beyond fatigued, and it wants to clue me in. I look down at my hands, gripping the stroller handle tightly for support, and think, *Well see? No shaking. We're all good here.*

But later as I help Charlie out of his jacket, my hand clatters on the zipper. I stare into his brown eyes and then bring him in for a hug. I'm shaky all over. My self-confidence as a mom of a small baby is shaky. My faith is shaky. My belief in whether the sun will come up tomorrow and that we will all do this again is shaky. So, in a way, it's good I can only see evidence of this in my hands because if my insides would match my outsides on this cold autumn day, I should be in a straightjacket.

For the previous six months or so, my depression and me had side-eyed each other. I felt much the same about this nemesis as my boys do when they are fighting, and I make them hold hands. They will slide over to each and limply hold onto each other as if the mere touch of the brother's fingers would sap all their energy, poutily waiting for the "Okay, fine, you can let go now—*but be nice*" from me. It's a great parenting tactic, enforced love.

I viewed my depression with sulky disdain. For one, I was already sleep deprived enough, why have the added benefit of depressive insomnia and fatigue? For another, what kind of mother beholds babies—really cute, blonde, brown-eyed little nuggets of cuteness like Charlie—with tired dread? I hated my depression. And so, for the months that it decided to come live with me, I avoided it at all costs. I smushed it down and ignored it. Sometimes I told myself, "Today, we are *not* talking with depression. He is a dork. We are just gonna have a *great* day and whatever you do, Dana, do *not* even go over there." Sometimes I tried to run, lift weights, and do these really intense exercise videos that made me feel like I was going to throw up right there in my living room if I did another lunge, so I could sweat the depression out of me.

I did go talk to doctors. I took a pill every night. And I drank a lot of water, tried to eat right, prayed, and usually felt better for all of it—for a while. Until my sullen friend would sit down on top of me at some weird point in the day and say, "You should die. You really should. Because nothing means anything. You will fail as a mom and a wife; you know this is true. And if you die, you will stop having me attack you out of the blue with a feeling of dread so deep it takes your breath away. If you die, you won't have to worry so much about Charlie getting hurt, dying, getting sick, or, God help you, having a tree fall on him or any of the other crazy fears you have about him at three o'clock in the morning. Other moms don't ever do this. So you need to get out now. Because it's never going to change, and you're never going to feel better. Not for real. Not for long. I will always be here waiting."

How in the hell are you supposed to argue with that?

Arguing *should* have gone this route: more prayer, more counseling, more visits with my pastors, more talking to Brian, and more pills, if needed. More waiting. The kind hearted type of waiting, like when you go to the hospital for a sick friend and you end up in the waiting room with some wrinkled *People* magazines and bad coffee. You don't yell at the friend for making you hunker down with the Worst Dressed list from 1999. You eat your weight in candy machine Twizzlers, and you wait. You play solitaire on your phone. You play Candy Crush. You then realize you are actually using a phone, and you make good use of your time and call your mama. You *wait*. It sucks a little, but that's what friends do.

I don't like waiting. So, I adjusted my argument by adding one ingredient: wine.

Every day.

Initially, there was some trepidation. I was still breastfeeding Charlie, so there was quite a bit of waiting, and timing, and the mental gymnastics necessary to make sure my boy was not going to be drinking his own after-dinner cocktail right along with me. And so it became just another "thing I had to do" for my child. Mothering was so hard. Mothering meant I had to have a glass at night. I had to. Because it was so very hard to figure out *how* to have that glass in the first place, so I just had to. Thus, the lovely Gordian knot had started to tangle and wind around my wine glass, my child, and me. If I drink, I will feel better. And then I will feel horrible because mixing drinking and babies is bad. So now I feel bad. So—I need to drink.

I get kind of seasick even trying to figure it out myself.

And so, each night as I started dinner preparations, I would pour myself—very carefully—one beloved glass of white wine. The liquid would cascade into the glass with a sweet golden fragrance, and something in me would unhook. It was as good as kicking off the heels and getting into jammies at the end of a long day. It was better. The first sip gave me hope that tonight would be warm and pleasant, not waiting, breath held, for Charlie to cry, or for me to burn dinner, or for Brian to frown at something I said. I paired burning the gravy with being doomed forever. Depression liked to amplify everything in me. It made sense, I guess, because I was stretched tight like a drum with every perception of what others were feeling or thinking about me pounding on me like I was a trampoline of crazy.

There is also the remote possibility that drinking that oh-so-holy glass of wine each night had a slight effect on the amplification. Yes, it probably *amplified* it. It's similar to the classic parody *Spinal Tap* when Nigel Tufnel explains that his amplifier goes beyond the usual "ten" on the knobs, and he proudly says in his British accent, "These go to *eleven*." That was me. I was so bloated with feelings and insecurity and pinging thoughts that I went to eleven. And the lovely warm swirls of liquid courage I waited for each evening? They turned the amplification down to a soft murmur. They took away the metal death band in my head and replaced it with something soothing, like Chopin. Or Veggie Tales Lullabies, since being a mom had sucked any sort of sophistication out of me long ago.

Nine months in, the depression lifted. I am not sure why, and I don't really need to ask. I am just glad it left. I woke up one morning, and the sun was actually shining in the windows. I started to see my boy with clearer eyes, and I didn't clench up with fear every time he squeaked. I didn't run to him with my breath held every time he cried. I stopped eyeing the baby monitor like it was the red phone in the Oval Office. Instead, it was just a baby monitor. And my baby, well, he was just a baby. He cried, was sad at times, and didn't always sleep very well, but he no longer seemed to telepathically shout: "*I am not gonna make it with you as my mom*" every time I picked him up.

He was a baby. My baby. And we were finally getting into a groove with each other. I was sleeping better. My appetite had returned. I had a picture of me back then that showed a mom who was laughing, holding her child, and speaking into the camera. My eyes were brown and pretty calm. Probably also a bit tired, but they crinkled with laughter at the edges. I was not wide-eyed with the look of someone in a police lineup. I was back.

And all I did, to celebrate, was drink more.

The problem here was that I had taken on my de-amplifier as a soothing answer to everything. My glass at the end of the day now solved *all* feelings, not just the bad ones. I was finding that I didn't much like feelings. They were a nuisance, and life was much more doable as a numbed-out Zombie mom, shuffling along to an ominous soundtrack with a kind of lurching fixation on five o'clock. The good news here, I guess, is I hadn't gone full throttle, *28 Days Later*, snarling zombie. No, I was more of a humming, listless June Cleaver zombie. I gripped my wine glass or scotch and swore nobody would get hurt as long as I could drink. Every day. Just a bit.

The snarling part would come later.

TOP TEN MANIFESTATIONS OF A ZOMBIE MOM

1. She is zoned out. Children fussing or crying only makes zoning out harder, but a second glass helps this.

2. Listless humming of church songs or Yanni pairs well with Zombie Mom to help with the perception that she is totally on the ball spiritually.

3. Zombie Mom prefers to sit still. There's not a lot of walking, running, playing, or general messing around. Thomas the Tank Engine on repeat is a great background noise. The children become a bit zombiefied, too.

4. She often has glorious plans for dinner but zombies out and goes for mac and cheese. Nothing wrong with a little mac and cheese now and then, but Guilty Zombie Mom is a *monster.*

5. Eats and eats and eats. This, too, adds to Guilty Zombie Mom—literally. She is bloated and tired.

6. She sleeps with the couch on a regular basis. Husband is confused and jealous.

7. Finds bath time, bed time, and book-reading time to be so colossally hard that she considers letting children stay up until eleven so they'll fall asleep on the floor. Easier.

8. Wakes up every damn morning thinking, *I'll just drink this weekend. Not tonight. I need to cut back. My head hurts.*

9. By four o'clock in the afternoon, she has already decided she will drink. Guilty Zombie Mom roars, but she gets a glass before it gets too loud.

10. Has absolutely no ability to deal with guilt, crazy, annoyance, pain, or even happiness. Those feelings are too complicated. Zombie Mom likes to keep it simple.

CHAPTER 7

I Have Found Jesus
but No Clue

"Why are you trying to get into my office?" A professor of biology is standing in front of me. She is staring at me, then at the doorknob that I've been frantically jiggling and pleading at for the past few minutes. I stare back at her, and I see her eyes tighten. I'm afraid the booze is wafting off of me in fragrant waves, and I try to smile at her as brightly as possible to tell her I do belong here. I just can't find my office.

"Oh, hi!" I smile and laugh, waving my key at her as if it will magically set a spell on us both, but she doesn't even blink. In fact, she seems to lean in a bit, and then I see it, a slight . . . sniff. And then a furrowed brow.

I chatter on. "I keep trying to get my door unlocked, and it won't open, and, well, I was wondering if they changed the locks for some weird reason. Did they not want me to work today?" This is followed by some squeaky laughter on my part, but Furrowed Brow is not in the mood for comedy. She now tilts her head to the door, and says slowly, "You are trying to get into my office. That's my office." I'm completely not processing this because my level of fluster has just taken all my synapses and wrung them out like a wet sponge. I attempt to furrow my brow too, in solidarity, because really this would all be so much easier if she would just lighten up a bit, and I say, "Is it possible you and I share . . . ?" Perhaps she has access to this space along with me. As I don't normally teach in this building, my idea seems very rational, and I am now thinking *she* is the one who is lost.

This thinking lasts for about two seconds, until the last remnants of normal brain functioning return to me, and it finally becomes very clear why I'm outside this very locked door, trying to open it with my useless key.

I was on the wrong damn floor.

I take a deep breath and look down at my hand, still gripping my key with all the hope it rendered. Then I smile again, hoping, begging Dr. Biology Professor to just smile back at me. I don't even want to explain, it's so stupid. And since I am in the presence of total braininess, explaining seems, well, awful.

"Okay. Well, I'm such a flake!" I titter. And there it is: my calling card that I have been giving out lately to all my friends and family when I am forgetful, late, or acting just plain weird. "I had too much coffee this morning for sure! This is what happens when you have toddlers." The calling card always includes the coffee-toddler backup to gain sympathy and help impress good mommy status. Nothing wrong here. Just tired, you know, because of them. I can get away with this because my kids are adorable. Flakiness is now permitted, and I can sidle around a real apology or explanation. It's the toddler cop-out; it covers a multitude of sins.

Except Dr. Frownie is still silent. I immediately decide she never had children, and she is terrible and bitter. I must be really bugging her with my adorable children excuse because she still *will not smile.* She just tilts her head toward the door again and looks at me, furrowed brow so in place I wonder if she has a headache. And then, I realize, I am standing in her way. She needs to get into her office. And I really need to leave this endless conversation and walk my useless self upstairs. Somehow I mention about three or four more humorous quips as I leave, trying to keep what is left of my dignity from keeling over right there in the hall in front of that damn door.

Stupid door. Stupid key. Stupid, stupid, Dana. Dumb, d-u-m-b. How could you? I listen to this chant as I trudged up the steps and then duck into the bathroom. I don't really care if I'm late. I am too dumb to teach anyhow. In the quiet of the bathroom, I lean over the sink and stare at the mirror before me.

My hair is in a smooth bun. Red lipstick. Black cardigan. My teaching uniform is in place. I am Teacher Momma, tidy, prepared, and ready for a classroom full of college kids and today's analysis of Walden. I have baby wipes, highlighters, and some Craisins for low blood sugar in my satchel. I have papers graded, extra Sharpies, and hand sanitizer. I am on point.

Except—I am also really, really hung-over. And that's probably why I couldn't figure out what floor I was on, or how to really talk to the rather irritated professor, or how to look at my eyes in the mirror.

Today, I look.

And then I take a breath and head out the door to class. I don't have time for any more horror shows this morning, and the mirror is previewing one.

Drinking had become a daily thing, but my amounts were slowly increasing. I had gone from my beloved two glasses a night to more like three or four, with some added scotch or even a tequila shot or two if it was a Friday. I don't really know when I started drinking more; I just know that the bottles were piling up in the recycling, and that some mornings my body felt beat up, like a strung-out boxer after a lost fight. I would rise, pour myself a big fat cup of coffee, and lean against the counter, praying for my boys to sleep in a bit longer before our day began.

Sure enough, my prayer would be answered with the soft thumping of toddler feet on the stairs, and I would mutter, "Thanks," to God for His sense of humor. God had a wicked sense of timing with me lately. On the days I taught, it always seemed, He would create more chaos, lateness, or even sickness for me to hurdle before I made it to my classroom in one piece, looking all smooth and coiffed as the consummate professional. I was beginning to get a little bit tired of God's handling of my life. Lately, everything had been so stressful and just plain hard.

The boys were leaning full into their tiny ages; they were squirmy puppies with sudden and strong personalities. And I was so tired all the time; I had no patience with tantrums or whining, and lately it had felt like Charlie, Henry, and I hopped from one storm cloud to the next. We did have brief sunshiney interludes, like a peaceful morning at the park, but too soon some epic battle would occur over a swing set, and I would find myself thinking, "Well, there you go. The day is ruined."

I had accepted the job as an adjunct professor at a local college. I hadn't been working since Henry was born, and I was giddy with the prospect of a writing position in academia—a sunny, tree-lined walk from home. I was teaching again. I could have intelligent, academic conversations about literature, libraries, and thesis statements, and no one would interrupt me by shouting, "I need to go poopies!" while I was explaining my view on anecdotal evidence in research papers.

I relished the job, doted on my students, and regarded my teaching time in the classroom as a sort of "me time" because it didn't involve timeouts or anything to do with baby wipes. I was teaching again and afterward I clicked home on my high heels and made snacks, baked bread for dinner, fixed the toilet, and fed the cat.

I could clearly do it all.

Except, when I couldn't.

Lately, my teaching seemed uninspired. My house seemed to be dusty and conquered by small, pointy toys. My cooking was mushy. My children were going through a stage that I called "search and destroy," and our appliances, and the cat, were not faring well. My sex life had waved a white towel over its head and was taking a long nap. Brian and I had the "two ships passing" thing down to a science, and neither of us were willing to talk about it. We were two very non-sexy, non-talking ships, and I was too tired to care.

Every now and then I would fuss about it. I would sit at the picnic table in the backyard, ever-present glass in my hand, and talk to God. These conversations often sounded like a script from *Days of Our Lives.*

Me: I know. You love me. You've always loved me. I just don't believe you anymore.

God: Yep. Always. Do we even really need to discuss this again?

Me: I just . . . It's just that . . . I don't know. [*Looks away with feeling. More tears.*]

God: I have never really watched this soap opera, so what am I supposed to do next? Look at you longingly? I really just wanted to talk to you about your drinking today. No drama.

Me: *See?* You don't even know. You want too much from me. We just can't make it work. [*Heads for the bar, which is my kitchen. I don't have a cool bar with pretty bottles and lead crystal, like they all do in their mansions.*]

God is all good, all the time. To most, this is an attribute, but lately, I didn't want to be hanging out with the big kahuna of goodness. I kind of just wanted to be left alone. I just wanted, really, for it to be five o'clock as soon as my eyes opened in the morning. My five o'clocks were shrugging back to four, and then three. I leaned into that time and that cork being pulled out of the bottle with a satisfying pop and a deep longing. And talking to God was nearly impossible because my prayers had always been so centered on me, and all I wanted to talk about these days was how brilliant and intelligent the inventor of boxed wine was.

I wasn't really on speaking terms with Jesus either. This was simply because He made me uncomfortable; it seemed that every furtive slide into a church pew these days was loudly followed with a big long sermon on Jesus's death. He died for me. On a cross. Yes I know. I believed. I even loved Him, but there was no way I could pair up my growing addiction to a boxed liquid as something I could choose over Him. But yet, I did, every day. So, instead, I would just sigh in defeat and scrunch down in the pew. My prayers sounded like this: "Okay, Jesus, we need to talk. I can't seem to quit the vino. I think I might need help. And yes, I know being lashed to a cross because of me is really intense, but I would prefer, actually, to not think about that right now. You died so I could drink boxed wine? That's where I'm at right now. I need to talk to you, but I'm so utterly underdressed. It's like trying to get an appointment with the president and wanting to talk to him about the pothole in front of our house. Our agendas are not matched. Please help. I need your agenda. I gotta quit the wine. But, I just don't want to."

That would have been okay to tell Him all that. I bet He knew it anyhow—since He made me and all—but numbness and zoning out were becoming my main mode of communication now. I had decided that this world had become difficult to interpret, like I had been lifted up and transplanted in the side streets of Paris again, and wine in copious amounts made me speak fluent French. With a wine glass in my hand, I could handle the accents, the customs, and all the weirdness of life. Without it, all I had was Jesus, and we weren't speaking.

I was not willing, at this point, to admit I had a problem. But each night, the glasses increased. The glasses became large plastic tumblers because I kept breaking the glasses. The boxed wine was like my own constant concession stand of mellow in my fridge. The wine was sweet and easy. It told me I was fine. It told me, also, that I was beautiful, smart, a fabulous mom, a chef, a baker, and a candlestick maker. It was my best friend.

All the while, my fabulous afternoons were met with rather ugly mornings. And after about two drinks, my overzealous plans to reorganize my pantry or groom the cat were buried under a sleepy haze. I wanted only to be numb and smooth, but wine was starting to fail its job. I lived in the rough crannies of self-loathing and self-adulation. This is the paradox of alcoholics and addicts. We hate ourselves; while at the same time, we are creating our own manifesto of awesomeness. We want only to be given endless attention, yet we shrink from it when offered. We love to navel-gaze, but we hate our increasingly pudgy navels. My ego had me trapped, and the only thing that improved that tenuous relationship was more wine.

I am simply the worst mother on the planet, but still so very important.

Hyperbole was my new home. It was uncomfortable except every day between the hours of 5:00 p.m. and 8:00 p.m. Then, all was forgotten. And forgiven.

TOP TEN WAYS TO TALK TO
YOUR HIGHER POWER

1. Just so you know, I don't believe in you, but I am gonna try this anyway. I've got nothing to lose.

2. I don't believe in you, but I have to talk to you. I have lost everything.

3. I believe in You, but I'm angry. And no one else will listen.

4. If I talk to you, will you keep it all to yourself? I heard there are rules. I don't like rules.

5. I want to try something new. So, here we are. So, how are things?

6. Really. I'm fine. But if I wasn't fine, could you help?

7. Two nuns, a priest, and an alcoholic walk into a bar . . .

8. Maybe I'm not fine.

9. Help.

10. Please.

CHAPTER 8

Pinball

Dealing with toddlers on a regular basis is like that whack-a-mole game we played as kids at the carnival on summer nights. Some skill is involved but mainly just proximity and tenacity. Dealing with toddlers while blitzed on boxed wine just gives you a headache and a hatred of moles.

I am sitting in our sunny playroom, watching my boys construct endless train tracks, and wondering how the hell I got here.

I want to fix myself a drink. It would be a nice biggie-size orange juice with a biggie-size dollop of tequila. As it is ten o'clock in the morning, the orange juice saves me a bit. It's like attending a yoga class only to binge on McDonalds on the way home. The yoga makes the fries and triple shake acceptable, in a very blessed, mellow, yoga pants kind of way. Same with the orange juice. It makes the tequila just an accessory to all this. But, as my rule stands, drinking in the morning, or even before five o'clock, means I am one of those stupid "problem drinkers." These people are unintelligent lush balls, and I'm not. I graduated with honors—a fact I like to remind myself of whenever my sad heart starts to fuss. I use it often, once after what we call the colossally Bad Ham Incident of 2012, but Brian doesn't really get what my college days have to do with gluey red-eye gravy.

And in my there and then, there was a lot of thinking about drinking. I would wake up, feeling rather crusty and stuck to the bed. I would stare up at the ceiling, watching the fan above us rotate, blinking with dizziness. My brain was wadded up against the back of my skull. Then, two small ravenous toddlers would wake, and my day would start about as peacefully as the revving up of a loud chainsaw. I would sit up, and then my brain would slide and settle with a painful thump. My morning was then punctuated by large mugs of coffee and a few conversations with my soul that went something like this:

Me: "Hi. I feel like shit. Let's not drink tonight, okay?"

My soul: "I am not available today. In fact, I'm on permanent leave. You're on your own."

Me: "Fabulous."

At that point I would choose my route for the rest of the day. Route one involved me becoming, with help from a lot of coffee and a lot of sugar, Super Perfect Mom. My kids and I would run errands, go to toddler time at the library, and even attempt crafting with glitter. To this day I wonder if it wasn't the glitter that pushed me over the edge. I would whirl about, smile, and somehow manage to have my crap together to the point that if other mothers were having a hard time at playgroup, I would just wander over next to them with my fully stocked diaper bag and offer them a healthy snack and some good will. I was Super Perfect Mom, able to conquer two toddlers and stock every moment with educational memories. I would collapse around three o'clock and then start drinking by four, which is an hour before my legal time, but I deserved it.

Route two was deciding that my headache was in charge and packing it in for the day. I would stay on the couch with my laptop and surf Old Navy and watch videos about cats riding vacuums. I would also eat a bunch of Swiss Rolls and hide the evidence from my children, as those things are horrible for you. Did you know you *can* stuff an entire Swiss Roll in your mouth at one time and then tell a toddler to remember to flush the potty? It's true. The toddler might be a bit confused by your sudden speech impediment, but the meaning is clear. "What's that, Mommy?" Charlie asked as I tried to swallow.

"It's spicy," I said.

Many route-one days led me right to route-two behavior. Route two also meant drinking by four in the afternoon because I am a horrible, slothful person with children who are going to go brain dead from watching too much Caillou, which we all know is a carcinogen. So I might as well.

"I might as well" was something I used often, too—almost as much as the "I graduated with honors" deal.

Every once in a while I would wonder if my drinking was a problem. But then, that wonder got buried under a child screaming about his Thomas the Tank Engine stuck behind the radiator, or a bill arriving and seeming so huge I was surprised the mailman was able to carry it to the mailbox. The medical bill we received for my past C-section was so colossal

I wondered if they messed up and thought we had triplets. Incidentally, if you ask for some Vaseline at the hospital because your lips are chapped, and there is no lip gloss anywhere—even though you asked your husband to bring you one of the forty thousand tubes of the stuff at home, but he was tired and forgot—*the hospital Vaseline costs as much as a car.* An economy model, for sure, but still. Vaseline, evidently, has the chemical make up of smeary gold, at least to the hospital people who price the stuff.

Every time I figured that I would try to forego—just tonight—a drink or six, *something would happen.* Some toddler incident would occur so mind-bending and whack-a-mole-ish that I couldn't see survival of this event without brown liquor or wine from a box. I didn't need even the lovely sound of a cork pulling out of a bottle to lower my blood pressure anymore; the gurgle and pour from the wine box into my plastic cup was enough now. And since all toddlers have the capacity to create havoc and keep popping up all over the place, my scotch and my wine were the only effective mallet I had.

"Tomorrow," I would mutter, as my little crazed rodents squealed and played in the other room, and I would glug another glass out of the refrigerator. "Tomorrow is another day. I'll worry about that tomorrow." I had become the Scarlet O'Hara of alcoholism.

"But for now, I might as well."

As the drinking increased, so did the depression. You'd think someone who graduated with honors would be able to see the correlation. My days were filled with manic mom behavior, fatty food, and a lot of online shopping. I was desperately searching for anything I could find to help me feel better. My bedside was littered with self-help books like *Conquer Your Fear and Anxiety in Three Days!* and *Why So Glum? Depression Be Gone!* The trash can by my bed was full of Mike and Ike boxes and Hershey's wrappers. The television was always on, providing a comforting low roar. I was like a pinball looking for any type of fix—food, psychology, Nordstroms.com, anything—to help ease the ache in my heart and head. The most basic answer was right in front of me: get rid of the glass in my hand. But I wasn't desperate enough.

My health was deteriorating. So many days were spent with ibuprofen and water and endless miles on the treadmill, hoping to purge my system and set the refresh button each day. But renewal on a forty-three-year-old mom is not easy; our bodies are made for charging after small children, missing nights of sleep, and fighting off a million germs on a daily basis. Pile on top of that the daily intake of large glasses of both clear and brown liquors, and my body pretty much threw up its hands in surrender. Literally.

Sleeping had become a new battleground, and I was losing at that as well. I'd always loved to sleep. I loved comfy pillows and heavy down blankets; I really loved my ceiling fan that hummed along with my dreams. I even loved the snoring lug next to me who'd sometimes kick me in the middle of the night in his dreams of old rugby games. I loved to curl up against his warm back and sigh into slumber, hoping it wouldn't be a rugby night. I loved sleep.

Funny thing about toddlers: they don't love sleep nearly as much as adults. However, the biggest problem I had now was nightmares—dreams of such epic, movie-like quality I swear some of them came with their own soundtrack. They had

Oscar winning plot lines with characters that came straight out of a Quentin Tarantino movie. The dialogue was riveting. There were special effects involving lasers and space travel, but their main theme was that they were utterly terrifying.

My dreams had two motifs: running from and running to. Most nights I would be running from a whole tableau of lurching, bloodied monsters. But worse were the ones where I was frantically looking for, or running toward, a loved one, only to find them gone, lost, or, worse yet, disinterested. My nights were fraught with longing and fear, and yet, in the sunlit hours of the day, I was never able to make the connection to my petrified state while awake. I searched for someone to love me, but all I could find was some liquid in a bottle. The inadequacy of this love was slowly driving me crazy but not in a way I could acknowledge in the daylight.

One night Brian woke to find me at the bedroom window, staring down at the street below. He sat up sleepily and asked, "What are you doing? What's wrong?" I didn't reply for a long minute and continued peering anxiously up and down the street. I was looking for shadows, for lurching figures to form in the darkness, and I was planning.

I spoke over my shoulder, "Do we have any wood?" Brian just sat there and blinked. This was not really his thing, having conversations about our lumber supply at 3:00 a.m.

"Wood? Uh, why? Come to bed, honey."

"We need wood to bar the windows." I placed my hands on the cold glass and craned my neck. Outside was our yard, our front walk, and the tree-lined street—all lit by the moon. I was panicked.

"Sweetie, you're dreaming. Come to bed."

I didn't come to bed. Brian fell back asleep, but I walked up and down the hall on a 3:00 a.m. march of desperation, planning our survival for when the zombies would attack. Some would say I was sleepwalking, but I remember everything that night. I was awake—washed up in a horror-movie haze of many glasses of wine—but awake all the same.

TOP TEN PHYSICAL SYMPTOMS OF EARLY ALCOHOL ABUSE

1. Joint and muscle pain. The kind that happens when you first wake up and try to walk down the hallway, and suddenly you realize you are sixty-three years old. But you're not. You're forty-three. This is confusing.

2. Headaches that ibuprofen will not touch. Extra-strength, maybe. It feels like your brain is sloshing about in your skull because it seems to have gotten too large. This headache is often accompanied by two toddlers who like to play the drums.

3. Sleep apnea. Scary stuff.

4. Sleep walking. Full-on anxiety manifesting in nighttime tours of the house, or worse.

5. Sleep that's not really sleep. It's a troubled, wet sheets, fraught-with-anxiety shift every twelve hours or so. It's a terrible thing to dread sleep.

6. Stomach problems. Of course. These are usually combatted effectively with a large coating of grease from double-size fries and a shake on a daily basis. This leads to:

7. Weight gain. Bloated tummy. Bloated everything. Which leads to:

8. Depression. Self-loathing. Low self-esteem. Rinse. Repeat.

9. Lower back pain in the area of your kidneys and liver. Often this leads to more drinking because just thinking about what your internal organs are trying to do to filter all that booze is awful.

10. Fatigue. Not the "I just walked two miles, and I'm tired" kind, but more like the "I have to cash a check at the bank. And then make the boys' lunch. This is not possible. I cannot even comprehend driving, and the whole teller thing with the slot and the check and putting the kids in the car. I'll do that tomorrow. I'll feed them tomorrow" kind.

CHAPTER 9

The Dog Dies

I'm at the library, browsing for something fun to read. I can no longer handle the classics or anything that has sadness, children who are sad, or children who *might* be sad at some point. My options are limited. I've noticed that since I had babies, all I can check out are bright pink and yellow chick-lit books about shopping and sex in New York, not really a genre I can relate to, but they do the trick. I do see a copy of *Marley and Me*, a book I've wanted to read for a long time. I mean, look at the adorable cover! The librarian agrees with me as she checks it out but then says, "Such a great book. Cried all through it." I stare at her, and she adds cheerfully, "The dog *dies*."

Daily drinking has now taken over. Completely. My amounts have escalated into a bottle or more a day, and at times I'm so drunk by the afternoon that I am unable to properly care for my boys. How did I get here? How did this happen? My life is so fruitful and blessed; my boys are adorable and loving, and my husband is a kind, gentle man who is fully devoted. We have a lovely house, lovely friends and yet . . . here I am, leaning into wine and booze at four or three o'clock each day, with dread and need.

I am hiding wine bottles in my home. Some are upstairs in my closet, tucked behind folded jeans or safely hidden inside my cowboy boots. Some bottles are nestled in the laundry baskets by the kitchen. A few are behind my easy chair in the office. It's possible there are more elsewhere. I have forgotten. I do this because I really don't want my husband to know how much I am drinking. At this point, he is pretty clueless—or so I think—and I want to keep it that way. I plan to stop drinking so much once the holidays are over. Or after my birthday. Or perhaps once there is a warm-up in the air; I can't endure the cold, dark winter nights without a glass or two of Zinfandel.

Christmas is coming. This means eggnog, Baileys, and bourbon, or perhaps a nice cranberry martini. All of these ideas make my eyes brighten because I find no pleasurable anticipation in anything except the thought of my next cocktail.

Any time I face the awfulness—that I'm hiding a solid addiction to alcohol behind a pretty cover of a peppermint drink recipe from Pinterest—I cannot bear it. "Lord," I pray, "I will stop. I know it. But please, not yet. Please . . . don't take away my wine."

And then, later, "God. I'm sorry. I just . . . I need it. Please forgive me. I think I might need this stuff more than I need You."

And finally, "I hate me. I hate all of this. But I have no choice. The alternative is too hard. Leave me alone."

Those prayers were few and quiet. They hurt so badly, to voice it all, that I mainly kept very still and didn't pray much.

Or, I raged. And the noise and fervor of it shouted down any chance of listening, so it worked well, too. One evening, my sweet husband had had his fill of coming home to a wife who seemed to be only half there. We were sitting down to a mediocre meal of Thai chicken, and I noticed him getting up to retrieve the salt. I found this unforgivable. As far as I was concerned, any seasoning of my meals meant I was the worst cook in the history of white girls trying to make exotic food, and he was going to pay.

"What are you doing?" I hissed, as he smothered his rice in more salt and some chili sauce. He blinked at me, and the offending chili sauce hovered midair above the sad chicken dish. I couldn't tell you if it was under seasoned or not. It so happens that scotch and soda at 4:00 p.m. kill your taste buds for anything else, unless it's more scotch and soda, so the chicken dish could have tasted like packing peanuts for all I knew. What I did know is that even if it did, Brian had no right to sprinkle salt all willy-nilly. It was, obviously, a direct attack on my ability to run a household. "I know what I'm doing," I barked nonsensically. "The meal is fine. Why not just dump it in the trash?" Brian was trying hard to understand how the salt had become a thing, but then I think he decided enough was enough.

The fight from that point on was a bit hazy because I decided to get really, really mad about salt. And he decided to get really, really mad back.

At the end of the argument, we had moved to the living room, and the boys were still in the kitchen throwing Thai chicken at each other. He glanced toward the kitchen to make sure they were out of earshot then said, "That's it. I am getting rid of the booze. No more drinking in this house until you can handle it, okay?"

He had said it. Finally. The drunken elephant had finally collapsed in the room. A part of me, way down, felt relief. But, as is common for me when faced with the truth, the best thing I can think of to do is run. We stared each other down. I tried to look like I could handle all of this—all the booze, plus no ability to reason, minus one husband, possibly. I tried to look tough. Solitary. Smarter than him. All this was hard work, and I think my face just appeared rather slack and twitchy. As both babies looked over the blandness and rice on their plate, I sobbed in anger, but also in pure humiliation.

I said, "Fine. But I am fine! It's not the booze that's a problem here, it's *you*." He ignored me as he grimly collected the precious bottles in one large, clinking box and took them away. I cried like someone had shot my dog.

I think of my drinking as a Trojan horse. It would move in, a grand gift, and I would happily numb out with it for about an hour. Then, all hell would break loose. It would attack everything that was good in my life—my marriage, my children, my house, and my ability to cook rice. But the very next day, I would invite the horse right back in through the front door. "For me?" I would smile. "It's perfect!"

The insanity that is prolonged drinking had hunkered down in our house.

One month later, Brian lost his job.

The next day, my beloved dog Norman died.

No, this is not a country music song. It had been a bad few weeks. Somehow I managed to think none of the bad stuff circling me was accentuated or rubbed more raw by my drinking.

I loved my dog. Losing him hurt; a deep, hard pain that nestled in behind my heart and seemed to say, "You're all alone now. He was always there, and now . . . he's not."

Losing Norman was like losing a link to my past, the one in which I was young, drank apple martinis, and still somewhat normal. And when we finally did take him in and told the vet he was no longer able to walk without groaning in pain, I realized how much I would miss him. He was always with me, a large, black, scruffy shadow with clicking toenails and terrible breath. And now, I was at the end of my tether. I thanked Norman's profoundly bad sense of timing for that.

My scruffy dog had been right by my side, to the best of his dog abilities, for eleven years. I had found him at a local dog shelter when he was about two years old. The sign on the cage said, "Terrier Mix," and he was *very* mixed. His wiry black fur stood up on his head, giving him a pointy Mohawk that fluttered in the breeze as he trotted next to me. I had taken him out of the cage to take a little walk with him. I don't know why. The name on his cage said, "Buddy," but he was so not a "Buddy"; he was a "Norman." I realized then that I'd already named him. He was almost fully grown and scruffy, like he had been in and out of a few juvenile centers. He had a *past.* But when he walked next to me and lifted his whiskery chin to the breeze, sniffing it with joy, I knew it. He was mine.

He would be with me for the purchase of my first little house, a hugely scary venture for me, and a solid step, I had thought, toward marriage with my boyfriend of seven years. Norman had been there when that marriage never happened, and the reality of that was so colossally surprising and painful that I didn't leave my couch for days. He had been there through the sleepless nights of tears and loneliness, of realizing that I had not been enough. He had leaned against me as I leaned into the fact that I now owned a house, one I had thought would be for "us," but now seemed to echo with the loneliness of "just me." He was there as I learned to mow my own lawn, deal with the sump pump, and pay a mortgage. He was there when I realized that cleaning the leaves out of gutters might involve dead birds, and he was kind enough to dispose of them for me as I screamed, "Ew! No! Ugh! No, no, *no*" and sprinted inside to douse myself in Lysol and a hot shower. He had snuffled his scruffy face in mine as I cried and watched *Pretty Woman* on repeat, always wanting to end up as Julia Roberts's character, without really coming to terms with the fact that she was a prostitute first. I fell deeper and deeper into the broken-hearted stereotype of someone left at an imaginary altar. Poor Norman. He had to withstand me singing along to Roxette's "It Must Have Been Love" so many times I'm amazed he didn't howl along.

He was with me when I found myself dating and dating and finding Jesus and not finding anyone else. He was with me when I realized desperation and wine go together quite well. I think he tried to tell me, many times, that I didn't need anyone so badly. That I could be alone. "After all," his brown eyes told me, "You have me. I might have dog breath, and I know I just chewed up your Doc Martens, but really, I'm not a bad catch." It was true. He was the king of dogs. He was there for both babies, when the only attention he got was, "No! No lick, Norman!" about thirty million times a day.

He was there when I sank into despair and when I bobbed along with all my afternoon glasses of numb. He was there for me through it and by it and with it. His large tail knocked over glasses, and he would step on my toes, but even after the chastisement and the "No Norman!" his whole body would swivel in joy if I scratched the fuzzy part behind his ears. He was there, while his muzzle turned gray, his eyes dulled, and he found the stairs to our bedroom too steep to manage without our gentle help. When he fell, twice, on those stairs, cold and wooden, I wept with him at the base of them. His trusting eyes still searched for mine as I stroked his head and looked at Brian with despair, knowing how I had to take a trip to the vet later, how I couldn't put it off any more. Norman licked my hand and said, "I love you. It's been good. We're best friends, always. And I am really, really sorry about those Doc Martens. I couldn't help it, you know. I'm a dog. And they tasted so good."

TOP TEN WAYS TO DEAL WITH REALLY BAD STUFF

1. Try not to panic or run around a lot.

2. Saying things like "Well, now I know how Jesus felt on the cross!" isn't helpful either.

3. Once again, throwing copious amounts of alcohol on top of bad things only makes them wet bad things.

4. Stop thinking that all bad things are your fault. Sometimes there is no karma; there are only bad things that happen.

5. Sometimes there is karma. If the bad things are your fault, own them and do the next right thing. For example, apologize. Or clean up. Or try again. Crying a lot doesn't help, unless you do it while you clean. That's okay.

6. It's okay to want to throw in the towel and sink into lumpiness and depression. Do that when you sleep. Throw that towel right in. But don't do it during the day because you have to walk and eat and probably feed little ones. Keep the towel throwing for bedtime. Make it fun. Add sex if you want; wear just a towel to bed and see what happens.

7. Or, throw in the towel for one day, and make it a movie day: popcorn, blankies, something fun to watch, and some chocolate—the remote always within reach. Do not choose movies like *Old Yeller* or *All Dogs Go to Heaven*.

8. Try to understand this sweet platitude my father tells me, "Life is hard. It is a bitch. Move on."

9. Find faith. I don't know how to do pain without faith. It's why I drank. If you can't find faith, ask faith to find you, and promise to wait.

10. Accept pain and then surrender to your hatred of it. Then, watch it lift. Surrender is hard but necessary. If you don't know how to surrender, pray like this, "Dear God. I have no idea how to surrender. So, please help me do it. Amen." Watch and wait.

PART TWO

The During

"Human kind cannot bear very much reality."

T.S. Eliot

CHAPTER 10

Measuring Time

Alcohol and me were really serious. We were totally committed to each other. And alcohol wanted me to end it with my husband.

I'm watching Brian make me a margarita. I'm happy he is willing to do so, yes, but it is maddening to watch. Brian is meticulous about things. He measures soap for the laundry. He measures his cough syrup out into those little plastic cups. Who does that? Don't we all glug it? And now, he is measuring out a cute little jigger of tequila for our margaritas, along with precise amounts of lime juice and Cointreau. It is our Friday night treat, a pitcher of margaritas and some guacamole. I had suggested it earlier as he drove home. "How was your day?" I ask, trying to pour a glass of wine, pick up Charlie, and talk on the phone all at the same time. It's a wonder I wasn't trying to talk into the wine. I have done this before to the tragic result of a big spilled mess on the floor. I was frustrated with the cleanup but even more so with the wasted wine.

"Fine," he sighs. "Long. Tired. What's for dinner?" I brighten because I already have this planned.

"Tacos! How about you pick up some stuff for margaritas?" I try to keep my voice casual and light. This is all just in fun—margaritas have to go with tacos, right?

I set Charlie down on the floor, and he immediately grabs my sweats and tugs. "Pick me up? Up Mom? Pleeeaaase?" I shake my head and he starts tugging harder, my sweats actually start traveling south, and I find my voice going up.

"And a bottle of white? I am thinking of making chicken divan tomorrow . . . for the sauce?" I am a liar. I wonder if he knows it. I don't even know what goes in chicken divan, but it sounds saucy. I know I will drink the bottle before then, but I can always replace it.

"Uh, sure. But I don't really want a drink; I think I'm getting a cold."

"Oh, okay. Well, no problem. I can just make some iced tea. Just thought it would be fun." I am at once heartbroken and incensed. I cannot imagine this night without a drink. It's Friday night. Friday nights are for unwinding, for fun, and for something to crack me out of this monotony and boredom. I can't stand the idea. I want to cry.

"Oh, I forgot! We have a little leftover tequila here—will you make me one of your famous margaritas? They are so yummy?" And I shut my eyes and lean on the counter, waiting. Please let it be okay. Please don't say anything weird. Please let me know everything is fine.

There is a beat, and then he says, "Sure. Right. I'll be home soon. I love you." We are well past the fight about taking all the liquor away. Liquor had found its way back into our house, and Brian was too tired and sad to argue with it, or me.

We hang up, and I survey the kitchen. Dishes are dirty, no tacos or fixings are anywhere in sight. And the whole leftover tequila comment was a total lie. I now have to bundle up the boys, get to a liquor store, *and* make a meal that is normal and yummy and warm—all in about forty-five minutes. I take a deep breath. I can do it. I am totally able to do it all.

Charlie and Henry are hustled out to the car, as they peep questions at me like little birds, "Where we goin'? Da store? Da one with donuts? I wanna donut? Canna?"

"Mommy just needs to go to her store and then right home, okay? Then you can watch Little Einsteins, and Mommy will make a yummy dinner." I glance into the rearview mirror as they sit in their car seats, chattering away like magpies. Henry smiles and kicks at the seat, and Charlie laughs. They are both so happy. Their eyes are clear and bright; they find the car ride fun; the car seats are fun; and the Veggie Tales compact disc is fun.

My eyes in the rearview mirror are shadowed and dead. I smile with my mouth at my children as they sing along with Bob the Tomato and then remind them, "Mommy will be right back." I walk like a zombie to the liquor store while they stay in the car, buckled and patient. We have done this before. I have always hated it, but I won't bring them in with me. I just won't. Leaving them in front of the store seems to be a better moral choice. It makes me swallow in disgust, so I purchase my numerous bottles hastily and speak cheerfully to the clerk, as if we were all fine, as if I were not in here every other day, as if all these bottles were for a fabulous dinner party.

As if everything about this is were all totally normal. As if my heart didn't feel like it were slowly turning to cement.

I slip into the car with my bag, ashamed and silent, as college boys and a few older guys pass us to go into the store. No moms seem to be here, and as the boys are still singing happily as I open the car door, I almost want to shush them—we don't fit here. But the boys are so happily oblivious that I feel relief. *See?* My brain says, *They're fine.*

And now I'm home, with tacos hastily constructed—keeping with my festive margarita theme—and I am watching my husband carefully measure margaritas with scientific intensity as I want to throttle him. He's preparing this drink for me like he's surrounded by beakers and test tubes, and I am going to drink it down in about three minutes. But it will certainly be delicious. I've already had a large glass of wine and a few tequila shots prior to his arrival, so he wouldn't know it was a new bottle. So as yummy as his drink may be, it will be lost to my booze-coated taste buds.

Lately my husband has been swimming through difficult territory at work, and asking him to bring home the celebratory bottle—"Hey! It's Monday! I hate them! Let's celebrate!" or "Hey, I'm done grading papers and only one third passed! I need to celebrate!"—often didn't pass anymore. More often than not my suggestion for a bottle of red was met with silence and what I thought was judgment that oozed out of the phone all over me in shameful waves. I bounced between embarrassment and anger when I asked, and when he dared to respond with, "Honey, didn't we talk about cutting back? How about some Chunky Monkey?" I wanted to howl with rage or slink away in contrition. I could never tell how he would react to my request for booze, and I was also never really clear on how I was going to react to his reaction.

This is why I started contemplating mail order. It is by the glory of my God that I never actually acted on this, otherwise there would be no book, and no Dana, for that matter.

It was an interesting way to live—so completely snowed under by emotions and then so completely numb to them. I was on that carnival ride that strapped you in and swung you perilously from side to side in a pendulum death grip. I found relief from all the extremes in my heavy pour of afternoon wine, but lately I needed more and more to even touch my feelings. It was as if the wine had decided I was too nutty to deal with and had sidled off into another party, where people were at least a bit less dramatic.

When provided with some nightly relief, no matter how muted, I still clung to it with increasing loyalty. It worked less, so I clung harder. Wine was a problem, so I decided I needed that problem even more. It was a bad boyfriend, and all I could do was continue my devotion in nutball Charlie Manson groupie style. The wine, in its own sickening pendulum swing, would give me dizzy relief for a few drinks, and then, within an hour or two, I'd be arguing with Brian, in tears, or asleep. Or a sickening combination of all three.

The thing is, I don't measure. I don't watch for levels or pour alcohol in jiggers, and I certainly hadn't been checking the barometer on my marriage. Sometimes I felt a cold lump of dread in my heart, and I wondered if measuring or what some call "moderating" my alcohol would ease it. But that was far too scary for me to think about for long.

I tried to moderate. It worked great for about twelve minutes.

So I kept hiding, kept rationalizing, and kept increasing for months. Brian was a fan of scotch, especially the really expensive kind. My first sips of scotch were with Brian when we were on a date. As he tried to tell me about the deep notes and the importance of the bog, all I could think was how it tasted like I was chewing on moss. This, I guess, is what you're aiming for when you drink the expensive stuff, but initially it just seemed a bit too fibrous and brown for me.

Flash forward a few years, and Brian's scotch had become a fallback to me—the "If there's nothing else, this-will-do-the-trick" drink. It was a hit of instant numb, and I grew to love its smoky flavor. If I could write a love letter to my alcohol, wine would be adored for its constant shoulder and its sweet okay-ness. A lot of mommies drink wine, right? So, no problem. Wine is the good guy boyfriend, the one the family loves, who is humble and so nice. Wine would be the boyfriend who would help me move my television or be there for a late night phone call when I'm sad. Dependable. Wine had no problem seeing me without makeup in my baggy flannel pajamas.

Scotch, on the other hand, hit me. And I just kept drinking it.

My husband was cluelessly patient. "Dana?" He would come into the living room as I dialed through Netflix, "Where, um, did all my Glenfiddich go? The good bottle? The one from my dad?" I had a variety of responses. Sometimes I went for a sullen shrug, which had never really worked for me when I was a teenager, but my husband was too nice to ground me. Sometimes I would simply act as if I had never heard of scotch before and had no idea what the brown liquid was over there. Most of the time, however, I would go for cute and pleading, all puppy-doggish with big "aw shucks, sorry" eyes, as I would come in for kisses and hope to distract him. Did all this behavior come up preplanned and intentional? No, I was neither that manipulative nor that smart. I leaned mainly on my feelings these days to lead my communication, and I did not necessarily mean to lie my way out of every instance. I loved Brian. I had just drained his ninety-dollar bottle in about three days, with absolutely no care about its woodsy top notes or whatever else the scotch tasters found so laudable about the brown stuff. I gulped it. It burned. It did the trick. For me, it was all about the end result, and Brian's precious scotch was simply a means to an end.

I have no idea why, one morning, I woke up and felt like I wanted all this to end.

But I did. My eyes opened, and I stared at that nauseating ceiling fan and thought, *I want to end.* Or, *I want all this to end.* I stared. The ceiling fan didn't stop, neither did the world, and I took a breath. My children were talking quietly on the monitor, and Charlie came down the hall, all soft feet and tousled hair. "Dood morning, mommah," he announced as he jumped up on the bed. I closed my eyes and reached for him. I decided I would stop drinking.

I would do it.

I would stop.

In three days.

TOP TEN WAYS ALCOHOLICS AND ADDICTS ARE IN DENIAL AND OTHER STUPID THINGS

1. When the recycling truck picks up your recycling bin, the noise of all the breaking glass is so deafening that neighborhood dogs start to bark.

2. On the flip side, dogs of the neighborhood love your trash because you're often throwing away entire meals that are burnt or rendered otherwise inedible due to schnockered cooking.

3. Your bank account is in a constant state of disgust or panic.

4. Your credit card bill reads every liquor store in the area with a highly patterned rotation.

5. You try not to cringe when Joe at your local liquor store shouts your name every time you slink in.

6. You are sure you watched *Survivor* last night. Really, you did. But strangely, *Survivor* is on again tonight. You wonder at your television's weird programming.

7. You don't watch *Survivor* tonight either. You sleep through it. You do remember arguing with your husband about a lost remote and that screaming, "The remote is your fault! I never loved you! This marriage is over!" was the glorious conclusion.

8. Contrition is not your strong point. So, you bake the husband some cookies the next day. But you burn them. See second point on the list.

9. You wonder if you'd feel less depressed if you (pick one or more): a) got a new hobby, b) got medicine, c) changed medicine, d) went on vacation, e) moved, f) tried belly dancing, g) got another degree, h) got another cat, or i) got rid of the cat.

10. You wonder if you should (pick one or more): a) drink only on the weekends, b) drink only after 9:00 p.m., c) drink only clear stuff, d) drink only beer, e) drink only things with umbrellas, f) drink only brown liquor, g) drink only one, or h) drink only three.

CHAPTER 11

The Big Tell, Part One

It was Thursday, after all. I couldn't possibly quit drinking on a Thursday. As luck would have it, Friday came after Thursday. Friday was for celebration. How I would deal with the *next* Friday I had no idea, but I hoped by that time I would have this all down.

I decided to quit drinking in a logical and healthful manner: I would go on a bender.

My heart soared. This would all be so simple! It was 9:00 a.m. on Thursday morning; I'd had my coffee, I was doing the right thing, and now I could just go out with a hurrah and be done with it! Why hadn't I thought of this sooner?

As is typical for people who are addicted to a highly poisonous and mind-numbing substance, I had forgotten about the nine gazillion times I *had* thought of this sooner and had failed. I had tried to quit many times before, or at least to cut back. When, in desperation, Brian had piled all the bottles up in a box and left with them, part of me wanted to go along with his plan.

Clearly this part of me was very teensy because by the next night I'd already gone on a full-surveillance guerrilla mission to find that box, and I did, no problem. He had hidden it in the trunk of his car. I snuck out while he had the boys in the bath and grabbed one full bottle and promptly hid it in my closet in one of my boots. And that part of me, that teensy tiny part way down, realized this was nuts—I was hiding liquor in my boots for Pete's sake—sighed heavily and waited for the drink.

That had become my life. Waiting for the next drink. I drank to cope, to think, to like myself or just tolerate myself, or to not give up. I drank because I wanted to kill myself and also because I had decided drinking would keep me alive. Not exactly Mensa material, but I was pretty pickled at that point, and I chalk up my crazy thinking to the booze.

Why I thought I would be able to just quit *now*, after a lovely booze-filled weekend, I don't know.

I wasn't ready to quit, honestly. Being "ready" to quit alcohol is a lot like being "ready" to have children. It's an outstanding idea, but it's not like your body just decides to go "Ding!! Totally ready! Come on, babies!" and you're all set. I had a friend at a meeting once ask me, "But Dana, how did you know you *wanted* to quit drinking?" She was six days off booze and drugs, and she looked like hell. We all do at the beginning. She had clamped down on sobriety and had that half-crazed Bruce Willis *Die Hard* look in her eyes. I looked at her and thought, *I need to be very careful how I answer here because I could say something that would push her over the edge and into a large vat of Everclear.*

Then I realized I might just be holding my wisdom in a bit too high of a regard. I gave it over to God and spoke the truth.

"I didn't *want* to quit at all. I just did. And I tried very hard not to think about it for twenty minutes or so at a time." She looked horrified and relieved at the same time. I patted her hand and said what every meeting goer had told me when I was six days in, "It gets better." I'd hated it when they told me that, and I knew she hated me a bit, too. But I didn't care because it was the truth and also because it felt a little good to finally pass it on to someone else.

So here I was, on Big Thursday, all clearheaded and ready to dance off to the liquor store in a brilliant free-for-all of healthy last drunken behavior. I point out here, again, that alcoholics and addicts bounce back and forth between nutty, dumb, and healthy like we live in a game of Pong. Actually, I lived in whatever emotion was dialed up at the time, which, that morning, was robust glee.

And Thursday continued on. I ate a healthy lunch. I even made myself some hot tea in the early afternoon. I did a bit of yoga. And then, around three o'clock, I got rip-roaring drunk, made a horrible meal, probably yelled at my babies, and fell asleep around 7:30 p.m.

Not bad for a Thursday night.

When Friday came around my glee had been replaced by a peaceful calm, the way you feel when a storm is coming in, when you are standing on the front porch and know you can just duck inside when it gets really bad. That cozy planning carried me through my day as I ate more carrot sticks and read *Women Who Think Too Much*, a book I'd started over a year ago but never finished. I wonder why?

I also wrote in my journal and made a long list of "Things To Do that Are Not Drinking":

1. Read the Bible. All of it.

2. Journal every day.

3. Run ~~three~~ five miles every day.

4. Eat more salads.

5. Lose twenty pounds.

You get the idea. I looked over the list and chewed on my pencil a bit. My head felt light. This was, after all, totally doable. But the list was so *dull*. Really, it was more like a list that maybe Mother Teresa had in her journal, but I doubt Mother Teresa ever once scrawled in disgust, "you are such a lardass!" because wine had bloated her like a pufferfish. But I could do it—of that I was sure. I just needed to have a drink first.

Two-and-a-half more days to go.

Around two o'clock on Friday, I was really eyeing that journal. And my kids. And the clock.

That brand new bottle of white was chilling for me in the refrigerator. I paced around my house like I were counting steps and couldn't settle anywhere. The boys were playing trains upstairs. I started a load of laundry. The radio blared something alternative and Christian, which is an oxymoron, but it helped. I always listened to Christian music. It made me feel better about walking around with a glass of wine at 2:11 p.m. And so that's what happened. I walked around my house with a wine glass in my hand. I decided tonight I was really going to enjoy my wine and if that meant enjoying it a bit today, too, well, then, even better.

And that's when God just up and said, "Enough. I have had enough. If you want to get drunk, I'll *show* you drunk."

And since God is really good at doing what He says, He did.

I poured myself a glass of wine. It was two days until my last drink, so I had shelled out the big bucks for a bottle that cost thirty-seven whole dollars. This was big town wine. I took a sip. My body, at that point, didn't really savor anything anymore. I was always shaky and tired, the top of my head buzzing with leftover hangover, and I couldn't think in clear sentences anymore. My memory was fuzzy and pocked with negative emotions—blame, paranoia, and worry. My heart was sick. The roots of my hair hurt. Guzzling detox tea and running four sweaty miles each morning were not working anymore. Nothing was working anymore. So here I was, with this bottle and two more days. I had a stash of gin, vermouth, and some olives ready for later that night, and multiple pretty crimson or clear bottles for later that weekend. It made total sense, somehow, to go out strong.

I took a second sip. And crumpled straight to the floor.

I don't know exactly what happened. I took a second sip and found myself suddenly so terribly inebriated that I couldn't stand up. Or speak. Or function.

To this day I don't know how to categorize this. What happened was a miracle because it was so epically bad. Of course, while it was happening I wasn't all that aware of God's direct intervention. I wouldn't have cared if Jesus had shown up at my front door with a direct flight to the Hazelden Betty Ford Center. I just wanted to figure out how to get up off the floor.

My children were playing in the living room. I could hear them laughing and squealing to the television. *They are safe*, my brain said slowly. *You are not. Get up. Get up!* But I couldn't. I stared at my legs and leaned back against the cabinet. I thought I might throw up, right there on the ugly linoleum. All I could do was concentrate on one breath in and one breath out. I swallowed bile, and hot tears filled my eyes and started streaming down my face.

Two sips of wine and I was so drunk I could barely see? How could this happen? Some say my body had simply had enough, and my tolerance was zapped like a burnt-out light bulb. Others add I was probably still inebriated from the day before and had moved on to a blackout.

These are probably true. But the real truth is that my heart was not strong enough to stop drinking. My plan to quit in three days was just another attempt at controlling what had become uncontrollable. The plan would not have worked, and I knew it. For some reason, God decided to step right into my mess.

I don't know why He decided to do so. I still don't get why He would find me important enough, really, to fix firsthand. This is usually when my husband likes to interrupt me and gently suggest I'm thinking too much again. All I know is that He did. His method was a bit terrifying. I was on the floor and couldn't stand. I could barely make a sentence. My vision narrowed to a point on the floor.

As kids, my sister and I had this great game we used to play at the pool called, "Let's see if we can almost drown." We would submerge ourselves slowly and then rest on the bottom of the pool, silent and watchful, just sitting there calmly and waiting each other out. The muffled sounds of glee and splash above were lovely and far away. It was a different universe, our pool, and I usually won.

But then, breathing was needed. And we would crash to the surface and join the noise and the sun. I always kind of liked it down there in the blue gloom and quiet. That day, as I stared at my ugly linoleum, I felt that same weightless gloom and silence cover me. My boys were echoing shouts so far away. Sunlight was gone. And I was, too. It was rather nice.

I wondered if the children would find me like this. I wondered if Brian would be sad, after all these weeks and months of horrible.

I wondered why I hadn't died yet. And so I raised my arm up over my head, got a hold of the countertop, pulled myself up to a standing position, and slowly punched what I hoped was my husband's phone number. I couldn't really see, and my usual act of squinting one eye closed—which was often how I'd ended up reading at night before I "fell asleep" or "passed out"—was not working.

In poker, a "tell" is a physical reaction or behavior that gives or tells the other players information about your hand. I had a hand of cards that finally needed to be thrown on the table in defeat. It was too hard to try and keep the cards straight with the booze anymore.

Brian never usually answers his phone at work. Generally it takes about two calls, one voicemail, and three texts to get him to call back. This is not because he's insensitive, but simply because the man is buried under so much work it's amazing he comes home at all.

Brian answered the phone on the first ring.

I breathed into the phone. He said, softly, "Dana?"

"I can't. I need you to come home. Now. Please."

I hung up and slid back down the cabinet. Generally, it takes Brian about thirty minutes to come home. He was home in ten, I think.

He opened the back gate and walked up the house. I could see the tip of his blonde head heading my way. I lifted myself up again and somehow managed to walk out the back door to him. He made this face that I never want to see again. It was a sort of head tilted, soft smile, so full of love and concern that it melted me. But it was also full of pity. So much of it, in fact, that I felt weighted by it. His face told me what I knew Jesus also felt. Pity and love. Because really, I was deserving of love but also, painfully, all the pity in the world. As much as we fight for pity and sympathy, we hate anyone to actually feel sorry for us. This time he did. And simply, so did I.

I leaned against our back shed. "I can't do this anymore," I said. "I just can't." I leaned down, breathing, hoping desperately for this all to change somehow—for it to all go away. To lift up, like the end of a Disney movie. It was normally at this time that I would take a drink to help with the lifting. But since I had only two sips today and was so sick and inebriated that I could barely stand or talk, I didn't.

Brian reached in to hug me, and I wrapped my hands across my chest and held on to myself, terrified. My hands gripped onto my sides and tried to keep me together. He wrapped me up for a minute, but I pushed back.

"I can't. I can't do this anymore." Not once did he ask me what I meant. He knew.

I took a breath, fighting the waves of nausea and fear.

"But, I just can't go to meetings. I don't want to. I'm so scared Brian." And then I stopped and realized the truth of all this. The past years had been nothing but a slow build-up of a prison, my own prison, built for this very day. I sobbed against his shoulder and allowed him to hold me up. "I'm trapped. Please, I don't want to go to meetings. Please don't make me go to meetings."

He held on tighter and said, "We will do this. Together. I promise. All of it. I'm not going anywhere."

My eyes met his. They were so kind.

I took a shuddering breath and said it—the truth— "I can't stop. But, I *can't* get help."

He held my hands. He placed them on his chest. And he said, "Honey, you just did."

TOP TEN FIRST STEPS TOWARD RECOVERY

1. Ask yourself how sick and tired you are. Ask yourself how much longer you want to be sick and tired. Realize you are sick and tired of being sick and tired.

2. Go the research route. Start reading books about drunks who got well. Stick with the classics: Anne Lamott, Glennon Melton, and Caroline Knapp. Pile up these books by your bedside and try to read them with both eyes open, not one squinted.

3. Understand that everyone's story is different. Yours might not be Caroline Knapp's story, but you are

curious. You are testing the concept. You are just
researching. Don't be afraid.

4. Think about not being afraid a lot. Think about how
    you would like to not be afraid anymore. Allow yourself
    to realize that not being afraid is actually possible.

5. Then, don't be brave. Allow yourself to be *really* afraid.
    Maybe look up twelve-step meetings in your area.
    Or counselors who deal with addiction. Or rehabilitation
    centers. Feeling terrified at this point is perfectly normal.

6. Look up more meetings and counselors or places to go.
    This time, write down a phone number or two. Record
    an address into your phone. Go back to Disney movies
    for a while. This is big.

7. Any time any of the above seems too overwhelming, go
    outside and take a walk. Or have a bite to eat. Or pray.
    Or call your spouse. Have a code word that indicates
    you are freaking out and text it to him or her. Just keep
    swimming. Watch *Finding Nemo* a lot.

8. Tell one more person. Tell someone you really love and
    trust. Tell them what you're doing, what you want to
    stop doing, and maybe tell them the deep hard truth of
    it. If you put it out there, outside of the walls of your
    house, you're a rock star and very brave.

9. Tell them you want to stop. But you can't.

10. And also, tell them maybe you don't want to stop at all.
    But you must. Tell them this because it's the hardest
    part to tell. Then stop and feel this feeling: fear lifting.

CHAPTER 12

Tattoos and Meetings

"You're in the right place." A man with a spider web tattoo on his bald skull is smiling at me. He has gorgeous blue eyes, which helps ease my conviction that he might try to kill me if I sit next to him. Instead he gets me bad coffee in a Styrofoam cup. And thus begins my first meeting in a twelve-step program.

The first day of recovery, I hear a lot of new terms: closed meetings, open meetings, tools for recovery, enabling, and gratitude. These first days I'm on autopilot and mainly sleep and go to meetings. I also learn to lean on the concept of one day, one hour, and one minute at a time. Relapsing is constantly on my mind. The main reason I don't is that I constantly hold onto my twenty-four-hour chip and keep repeating, through gritted teeth, "Go to meetings. Don't drink in between." The tattooed guy told me that, and I imagine that if I don't do what he says, he is going to have me iced.

Day one.

Morning is rainy and warm. My brain keeps pinging on a hangover from two sips of wine. I find the messy living room so depressing; I cannot bear it. I stay in bed without even asking permission. The boys play downstairs, and I hear them shouting and jumping from the furniture. They're not supposed to jump from the furniture. I don't really care.

Brian brings me some water and sits on the edge of the bed. He looks at me anxiously and asks, "How are you?" I can't help but feel like I've landed in some asylum for the mentally incapacitated. I'm still in bed. It's past ten o'clock in the morning. Brian is all quiet and nurse-like. Alternate universe.

11:00 a.m. I look up a meeting on the great interwebs. It is annoyingly easy to find about twelve meetings within minutes of my house. I can't make a decision. I don't think too much. I drink more coffee and then take a shower and get dressed. I move like I'm on rails. The warm water feels good. I make the bed. I keep going.

11:35 a.m. I can't find the coffee grinder. I burst into tears. Again. I realize I've been crying off and on all morning. My eyes keep leaking hot tears that don't feel connected to anything. I cry when I drink some coffee. I cry while I shower. I cry when I try to make my bed. I lean on Brian and cry some more. I tell him I'm scared. He listens and then walks me to my car. He offers to come with me, but the boys need lunch. I think, *Maybe I can skip this and go get a bottle of wine.* My stomach turns, but I get in the car and drive past four liquor stores on the way to the meeting.

11:55 a.m. I am early. I walk in and three men stare at me. The walls are yellowed with cigarette smoke. The couch is empty, and when I sit on it I sink so low that my knees are at eye level. This makes me feel about four years old. The men are of the long-haired, smoker's cough, grizzled variety. I am so scared that I feel like the palms of my hands will leave handprints on my jeans. My knee jiggles nervously, and then I listen as the meeting begins.

12:06 p.m. I realize I'm in exactly the right place.

1:00 p.m. One of the meeting goers gives me a hug as I leave. "I want to give you this," he says. He pulls a twenty-four-hour chip from his pocket. It is old. Very old. "This is mine. I want you to have it. This is the most important chip you will get. That's how we do this. One day at a time."

He hugs me again and I think, *This man is God. I am hugging God.* I have a lot more super-spiritual thoughts like this as my journey continues, but they are normal in these meetings. It's totally normal here to hug a smoke-riddled, tattooed man who's been married three times and can drop the F-bomb in threes in each sentence, and yet I realize I'm more at home with him than I have felt in a very long time.

1:12 p.m. I drive home. I cry while driving, when I pull in, and as I come in the door.

1:14 p.m. My boys shout, "Mommmyyyyy!" as I come in. Brian says, "Hey! How was it?" I am ticked off that no one seems more concerned. This is big. They shouldn't be playing Candy Land and texting on the couch. They should be having a prayer vigil or something. Everything seems off. I want to go live at meetings.

1:15 p.m. I realize that often what I *want* others to be feeling will not be what they *are* feeling. I wonder if this whole recovery thing is going to be possible. I feel like that scary woman in *Hellraiser* who has no skin. I am a raw flesh monster walking around in a fuzzy bathrobe with a gloomy disposition.

1:20 p.m. I give up on feeling and take a nap. Naps are the new wine. I will take so many of them in the next three days that I might be turning into a bear. Brian doesn't question it; he lets me sleep. This, in itself, is solid proof that God exists and that Brian is listening to Him. The boys come up every once in a while, eye me, and ask me things like, "Where are you? Wat doin' mommah? Can you read dis to me?" And I read the Berenstain Bears and some Thomas the Tank Engine, and I do not, under any circumstances, leave my bed.

4:00 p.m. A deep gloom comes over me. I think I might stop breathing. I look for another meeting.

5:00 p.m. I sit at the table while my family eats. I push food around and watch them. I cannot be a human without wine. I'm aching for a glass of it. It is hard to eat a meal while the mother sits there and cries, so I get up and leave. I think perhaps this was all a mistake.

TOP TEN WAYS TO DEAL WITH YOUR DAY ONE

1. Breathe in. Breathe out.

2. Get to a meeting, a counselor, or your pastor. Talk to someone who can listen objectively. If that scares you that's good. It's okay to be scared. Do it anyway.

3. Don't think ahead.

4. Don't think back.

5. Think about the next ten minutes at a time.

6. Be super kind to yourself. Take a bath. Take a nap. Get a sitter. Take a longer nap.

7. Eat chocolate. A lot of it. Watch a lot of movies.

8. If anything panicky comes up in your head, just say, "I will deal with that tomorrow." Go all Scarlett O'Hara on all of it. The world will wait until tomorrow.

9. Expect to be shaky, achy, tired, and terribly out of sorts. That's all normal. Your tummy might hurt. Your body will hurt. You will think crazy thoughts. All this will pass. Get in your jammies and hunker down.

10. Don't pick up a drink. Just for today, the only thing you have to do is not drink. You can be cross, ruin your diet, spend too much at Amazon.com, yell at the poor dog (or even the kids—just say sorry later and try not to use profanities), cry a lot, or don't cry at all. You can do whatever the hell you like *as long as you just don't drink*. Just for today.

CHAPTER 13

Toddlers at 4:00 p.m.
Are the Devil

"Hi honey; how are you? How was your day?" My husband, a picture of comfort and compassion in well-pressed Dockers, leans in for a kiss. I turn and snarl, "I would *sell* both my children for a juice glass of vodka right now."

Perhaps this is not the best way to greet your darling when he comes home from work. But since you have been trapped in a house all day with two small mind-suckers, and an ache for alcohol as deep as the Grand Canyon, you can only communicate in snarl.

When I was sixteen, my boyfriend and I were at the movies and had slipped into the seats of our favorite movie theater to watch *Fried Green Tomatoes*. I loved going to the movies. I had my popcorn and my Milk Duds, a cute guy to snuggle with, and a great romance to feed my very sensitive soul for the next two hours. I loved the velvet, bouncy seats and the sticky floors. I really loved the previews but noticed that this time they seemed rather violent and explosive. Imagine my surprise as the movie started and instead of comedic whimsy, I was faced with grim music and a gray landscape. *Where's the sweet whimsy?* I wondered. *Where are the tomatoes?*

We both watched for a good five minutes, trying to figure out how *Fried Green Tomatoes* could have an introduction that involved so much loud, pounding music, and guns, but then I figured it out. "Wrong theater. *Wrong* theater. This is that *Silence of the Lambs*!" David just sat there a moment longer, transfixed, I think, by all the creepiness. I yanked his arm, and we made it into our tomato movie. It was a bit of a clash of sensibilities, to go from cannibalistic serial killer to sweetness and light. Kind of took the fun out of it.

Here I am now, snarling at my husband, and again I feel like I've just walked into the wrong movie theater. This is just a bad mix-up. Drinking wasn't so bad. I wasn't so bad. Clearly there has been a mistake, and I'm supposed to be talking and laughing with my husband right now, a glass in my hand, and my eyes bright with hope and wine.

I growl and snarl a lot in early recovery. Here's why: *Recovery is freaking hard.* It will make you curse like a sailor and lay you down in fits of rage and crying—and that's just the first twenty minutes of your day. On top of that, trying to get sober with two small children running about underfoot is simply astonishing.

I am one week, one day, five hours and fifty-two minutes sober. My days are a combination of counting the minutes paired with anything I can do to take my mind off them. I feel like I'm running a marathon and have hit mile nineteen. Painful.

Slow. Moments of clarity and elation. Then, cramps again. I keep treading along, looking at the clock, wondering when this will all be over, especially those maddening four o'clock "witching hours" where I contemplate actually selling my kids for some Gordon's gin. If limes were included in the deal, I might have done it.

The toughest part was realizing that recovery would never be "over"—not if I was going to take it seriously. When you're a part of my club, taking out a lease on recovery is not an option. When I really thought about the lack of alcohol forevermore, it felt like I'd been told to clean the Grand Canyon with a toothbrush, while blindfolded. But every once in a while, tiny moments of peace and joy descended upon me and were so defined and real, they lifted me out of my canyon. I would focus on the higher horizon then, and just kept walking.

One afternoon, I was sitting outside with the boys as they burrowed in the sandbox and proceeded to get absolutely filthy. This was their favorite game. They liked to pack the sand into every available crevice of their clothes and skin, so they could then shake themselves off like wet puppies inside the house, and then my house could have sand packed into its every crevice, thus matching my children. As may or may not be apparent, I'm a bit of a neat freak, and this whole sandbox thing seems like a cruel lunacy, but it was there when we bought the house.

I sat and watched them smear grass stains on top of the dirt smudges, a nice layering effect. I'd made some chamomile tea. It was ninety-two degrees in our backyard; the mosquitos had figured out I was tasty; and I hate tea. I watched as Henry took a shovelful of sand, smiled gently at his brother, and tipped it over Charlie's head. I listened as the wails followed. I took another sip of the stupid tea.

And I was absolutely at peace.

It had been so long since I'd felt such simple happiness that I found myself looking around in suspicion, as if God was going to come down at any moment, smite me over the head, and tell me to snap out of it. Instead, Charlie smote Henry over the head with a Tonka truck, and there was some noise and interruption to my happy moment, but I didn't care. I had felt happiness, for about four minutes. It was *pure* happy—not induced by wine or tequila or some purchase at Target or by losing a pound on a scale. It was just happiness. Just . . . because. And I would take it.

I looked around and took a breath, walking through cool grass on bare feet toward two fussing boys. When I sat down in the cool of the shade by the sandbox and talked down the boys from the epic *Game of Thrones* betrayal going on, I still felt at peace. I had been feeling peaceful for over five minutes now. That was a record. Shadows from the trees danced with beams of sunlight across the lawn, and my eyes filled with tears. Peace.

Six minutes of peace is a long time.

It was long enough that later—when I had spilled hot tea (cup number three) on my foot, shouting, "Ugh! Tea is for *pansies!*" and looked around my kitchen with the crazed demeanor of a flesh-hungry zombie in search of something, anything, to feed me right now—I was able to remember those six perfect minutes outside, in the sun, with the mosquitos and the children. It helped the inner-nutball-zombie lady take a breath and head for a soda. I poured it with grim determination and added about twelve limes. I would go hunting for that peaceful feeling just like I used to go hunting for a buzz. If my luck was right, and I had any trust that my Higher Power was actually who He said He was, then it would come back.

It didn't come back any time soon. This is the part about getting into recovery that terrifies most, and understandably so. An old-timer would tell me, "All you have to change is everything," and I would cringe. Those sayings, the ones that were yellowed and tacked on the walls in my meetings, are spouted on repeat like song lyrics stuck in your head. Sometimes, I hated them. Sometimes, I wanted to shout back: "Oh yeah? Well! Okay, hows about 'An early bird catches the annoying fellowship member!' or 'Do unto others' right back at you, bucko. If I wanted cutesy sayings, I would go visit my grandmother's house." I wondered how "Leave me the hell alone!" would look on a lacy pillow, and if I should start working on that for Christmas.

But the deal is, the damn sayings were *true*. And they were *right*. And, as anything in recovery usually goes, the things that are true and right are usually the ones we should follow. I would have to "Easy Does It" myself into as many meetings as I could, and then I would "Keep It Simple" right back home. And the toddlers, it seemed, really liked these slogans. Let's face it, toddlers have totally mastered living one day at a time. My boys wanted to be first, like, all the time, so they were real cozy with "First Things First." It was all "Live and Let Live" each day. A good thing, too, for my boys.

We survived it. One day at a time. My boys had no idea how much I was gripping onto this slogan with every ounce of my non-boozed-up self. Toddlers live a day at a time; they're hardwired that way. I envied them. I tight-walked through my days of getting up, doing laundry, breathing, feeding the boys lunch, and then, oh the horror, dinner. I braced myself for four o'clock like it was a tidal wave of awful. I had so many triggers I felt shell-shocked, huddled in fear and rage, and then paranoia, while two small boys shouted and ran around me like in a G-rated *Apocalypse Now*.

It was so hard. Putting a frozen pizza in the oven took it all out of me, like the pizza were some sort of massive crucible, and when done, I would flop back down on the couch with a sigh. Opening packages was hard. Going to the store? Intolerable. Talking a toddler down from a fit of hysterics because his beloved Mr. Spots (a stuffed hyena) was having a bath in the washing machine? Impossible.

So, why try? Why? If it was all so hard, why did I keep on?

One afternoon, I snuck outside for about twenty minutes to work on the snarled bit of weeds next to our house we liked to call our "garden." It had been one of those epically bad, I-can't-even-brush-my-hair, it's-too-hard kind of days. I hadn't worn a bra in over forty-eight hours. Lunch for the boys had been popcorn and old cheese. I was bored, tired, and angry, and layering that on top of my already neurotic tendencies, my poor boys and I were left with nothing but a crap sandwich for the day. I'd been told in sobriety to stay ready for HALT—meaning, are you Hungry, Angry, Lonely, or Tired? This made sense, but I was more of a BAD ASS—Bored, Angry, Disenchanted, Angrier, Sad, and kind of Shitty. That day, I was all of these things. So in a last ditch effort to feel better, I went outside in the nearly 100-degree weather and started weeding an impossible garden. In hindsight, it wasn't the best place to start with feeling better, but I'm always one for going big.

I put on Barney, headed through the front door that I cracked a bit, and repeatedly told them, "Mommy is right outside, just open the door and call me!" They nodded solemnly, eyes drawn into the vortex that is Barney. I needed a few minutes in the sun to clear my head and to actually get something *done*. After attacking the weeds and brambles for a good ten minutes, I looked up at the front door, still slightly ajar with the hypnotic sounds of Barney emanating from inside. I peeked in the side window. Both boys were sprawled in front of the television like zoned-out yogis—feet up above their heads, legs splayed, and hands in namaste—watching with rapt attention. I'm not much of a Barney fan, but I will give him props for the total mindsuck he provided for my children.

I finished a two-by-two foot area of the garden and sat back on my heels, refreshed by the steam coming off the earth and the whole good earthiness of it. I was working in the soil. It was good, healing work. I had done *one* thing right today.

That's when I made the mistake of going inside. I should have left them in there, I swear. But, you know, motherhood. So I went back in.

They took a bag of jelly beans, left over from the Easter before and hidden away in the deepest recesses of my Tupperware drawer, and ate about half of them. It was right then that the sugar must have hit because they proceeded to throw the rest of the jelly beans all over the first floor of the house.

They also decided the jelly beans needed accessorizing, so they added real beans, the beans from the Spill the Beans game, a bunch of grapes, and some marshmallows. "Da marspellows!" my son greeted me cheerfully, "Dey are all over da house!" He gestured widely, and one stray marshmallow flew from his sticky hand onto the carpet. I don't know if it was anger at myself for lax parenting (leaving small ones unattended, even for only ten minutes, is not the best idea) or that my children were so gleefully unrepentant. I already felt my house slowly sinking under its mess and grime, and what happened next was what is technically called, "mommy losing her shit."

I started with crying and progressed from there to stomping around and yelling. I threw away many things, some of which did not belong in the trash at all. I found myself simply screaming. It felt, for a moment, like I'd lost my mind, but I found it again inside all this rage. It felt good to cry and pummel a pillow and to yell and throw and rage. It felt good enough to keep it up for a full six minutes or so.

It was a horrible tantrum. My children, I've been told, have no memory of it. But I have memory of it. I always will.

Within an hour, the boys and me were playing Candy Land. I had Henry on my lap; my son Charlie lay on the floor before me, happily plunking his playing piece along the road to the castle. I eyed them silently. I felt like the abusive lover, begging for forgiveness and offering roses and gentle promises. I was just as stuck as I'd been with the alcohol. Stopping drinking had taken the lid off of something inside me that I could not even begin to deal with—anger.

If I wasn't careful, my anger was going to destroy us all.

My usual reaction to all this would have been: drink. Drink a lot. Get out the glass, go for the box, and get a hold of yourself. That drink would've been a gift because it would've given me time. Time to neatly fold up and put away all my tangled thoughts, to dust off my hands, and voila, my feelings would be cleaned up and tidy!

Sitting on that floor I realized a few things:

1. I hate playing Candy Land.

2. Everywhere I looked things were messy. My house. My life. My feelings. The cat box. My marriage. My parenting skills. My hair. Always, my hair. All of it. So messy.

3. The whole getting-sober thing had a lot more to do with the mess of my life than it did with abstaining from alcohol.

I could have gotten up, grabbed my keys, and headed to the liquor store. It was minutes away—probably around six minutes. I could have, but I didn't. Instead, I texted my husband and then went back to moving my Candy Land token to the stupid, messy, caramel castle or whatever it's called.

"Help. Meeting. Please."

Brian was good at responding to monosyllabic requests, and he left work early, so I could go.

I attended meetings every day, sometimes twice a day. Meetings were the only time during the day that I could breathe, and that a part of me could match up with all the other parts. That night I cried in front of a room of twenty others until my eyes were swollen. I was so tired. And they listened.

It terrified me to get my keys, get in my car, and go to those meetings. Sometimes I would know no one there. I would avoid eye contact and sit in the back. Other times, the meeting was full of so many dear friends it felt like attending my own party. These parties were somehow more fun than I'd ever thought possible.

And so I went. For some reason, I went. I got in the car and drove, and talked and cried, and said the Serenity Prayer. The meetings linked my days together.

I linked sober days together. Slowly.

Mo, a beloved old-timer, always told me, "Just go to meetings. And don't drink in between." Mo was a surly guy, so I wasn't going to mess with him. I simply did what he said.

TOP TEN ANNOYING RECOVERY SLOGANS THAT ACTUALLY WORK

1. *One Day at a Time.* I like to abbreviate it to ODAT. That way when you say, "I had a tough morning, but you know, I was all ODAT on it," you sound hip and cool.

2. *Keep it Simple.* I have specialized in all things not simple for forty-some years. It is about time for simple. I started this by getting a subscription to *Real Simple* magazine but realized, much to my chagrin, that learning to crochet the perfect Thanksgiving-themed duvet is not the simple I was looking for.

3. *Live and Let Live.* This means to let people keep living around you. Even when you are not sure you are hip on that. ODAT, ya'll.

4. *Surrender.* I hate this one. Unfortunately, it's kind of necessary. That First Step is a doozy.

5. *But for the Grace of God.* A bit of a tongue twister, but it basically reminds us to stay humble. Next time you spot a mom with wine on her breath, humming "Margaritaville" as she weaves past you at parent-teacher night, don't get all judgie on her. Don't do it. Focus on you. Maybe it's her birthday. Or maybe she has a cold, and she slugged some NyQuil prior. Or maybe she drinks a lot. Which leads me to . . .

6. *Your Side of the Street.* Every time you realize you're focusing on others and their numerous, aching, annoying, horrible faults, stop and refocus on you. You have enough to do here.

7. *God Grant Me the Freaking Serenity.* It's really effective to pace while you say this through gritted teeth, emphasizing every *other* word *because* you are *ticked* off. Praying tersely is always good for a smile from God. He does listen to it all, even if you insert some bad words in the serenity prayer. Something I've never done.

8. *This, Too, Shall Pass.* I like to say it with a Monty Python accent, all "*None* shall pass!" So far, all the bad stuff has actually *passed*. Sometimes it's replaced by new and even more interesting bad stuff, but at least it has passed.

9. *Everything Happens for a Reason. But Sometimes that Reason Is that You're Stupid and You Make Bad Decisions.* This isn't really a recovery slogan. For one, it's too long. But I like it. And it seems appropriate for me.

10. *Expect Miracles.* Oh, friends. It's true. I promise. It's really true.

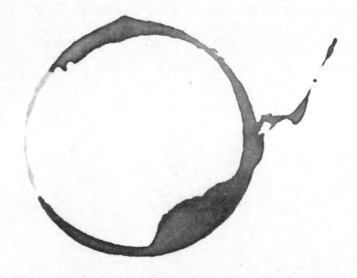

CHAPTER 14

The Big Tell, Part Two

"Well, I'm not pregnant. And I don't have cancer."

I'm trying to tell my dad that I'm an alcoholic. Dad is looking rather gray, so I decide to change tactics and go for the surprise attack.

"Um, I'm an alcoholic. Like you. So . . . me too!" I consider adding a weak-hearted, "Surprise!" with jazz hands. Luckily, my husband intervenes.

My father is an interesting combination of John and Bruce Wayne. He also has a bit of General Patton in him, but as he's gotten older I've seen less of that guy. He is so beloved and elevated in our family that we often speak of him in hushed tones—mostly when he's around because then we can make snarky comments about him since he can't hear much out of his left ear and refuses to get a hearing aide. This, I realize, is all his master plan. He is selective in his hearing. My mom knows this all too well. When we really want to talk to him, we hunker up close and yell things at him, like, "HI DAD, HOW ARE YOU? I MISS YOU!" And he responds, "Huh?" To which we repeat, "I LOVE YOU DAD. I HOPE YOU ARE DOING OKAY. HOW'S THE BUSINESS?" It's hard to yell, repeatedly, "I LOVE YOU DAD!" at someone without eventually getting irritated. It's all the yelling.

But that's part of the package with my dad. He's a combination platter of irritation, sarcasm, and deep, deep respect and love. I have faith in him. If I ever needed anything, he would provide it. I know this. He is the Old Faithful of our family. Timely. Responsible. Also full of very hot air.

My dad is, also, an alcoholic. He's in recovery and has been for many years. And now I needed to tell him about the fact that I am, too.

I felt like I'd betrayed him. All those years he'd told me, adamantly, that I was a "walking poster child" for joining his team. But I ignored it. I was too damn smart for alcoholism, for sure. Now I would have to explain how my smarts took me as far as my late thirties and how, after that, I'd pretty much traded in my brains for repeated refills of wine.

So there I was, in our kitchen, my dad standing before me. My mom sat at the kitchen table. My husband somehow maneuvered himself so he was standing directly behind me. If I took a step back I would bounce off him. He must have decided to take the expression "I'm here for you" as literally as possible, knowing how terrified I was to have this big tell with my dad. It's something I had dreaded since starting this whole process. Like going to the dentist, it was a virtuous decision but still awful in so many ways.

I'm wondering whether my dentist ever feels deep disappointment and betrayal at my lack of flossing. Then I realize I might be taking all this a bit too seriously. My dad loves me, quite a bit more so than my dentist, so I'm thinking he will be able to handle this information. He is a grown-up, after all. But I'm not so sure I am.

So, I tell him. And my mom. As I stand there and share the news, it happens. I lean back, and my husband wraps his arms around me. I did need him standing that close, after all.

My mom doesn't say anything. The kitchen lights glint across her glasses. She looks down at her hands, stoic, and seems perfectly fine. My mom has the strength and fortitude of one of those burros that takes fat tourists down to the bottom of the Grand Canyon and back up again. She has to. She's been married to an alcoholic for some fifty years and has seen her own share of grief and trouble. She deserves an honorary Emmy for standing by during all the drama with steadfast, tender faith. She loves us anyway. And, as ever, she isn't the one I am concerned about hurting. My mom will be all right.

"So will your dad," Brian reminded me earlier, numerous times in fact, as I fretted. "Your dad will be just fine. He will get all intense, like he does, but he loves you, Dana. It will all be okay. I bet he will lean in and grab your elbow like he does. He's good at that." I smiled shakily and flinched a bit. My dad is an elbow-grabber, yes. He leans in a lot, grabs that elbow right where the tendons are most tender, and somehow with his Vulcan Jim grip renders you speechless and completely still as he tells you, fervently, "Get the oil changed on the car, okay? Don't forget. And, don't forget to clean your gutters. If you don't, the whole foundation will go. Do you need any money? I got some. You need it? Oh, and mow your front yard, will you? There are leaves all over the damn place. You want me to mow it? I'll mow it." As I alternately shake my head no and nod yes, he leans in even closer.

"You doing okay? You all right?" And he means it. He means it on that level way deeper than the people you pass in the halls at work who greet you with, "What's up?" and move on down the hall before you can even answer, "Great! And you?"

My dad really wants to know the truth of it. I think it's because he's an alcoholic. He had surrounded himself with so much crap for so long that he's had his fill, and so now everything is unwrapped and very simple. If it's not the truth, it's not worth it.

So, in this moment, I am worth it enough to tell him the truth. Because he is in my kitchen and so is the gigantic elephant that I lovingly call "My Recovery," and we need to get it out of the room. It's crowded.

"Dad, I have to tell you something. Both of you. I have to tell you . . . " I take a breath and then decide to go forth and blurt it. This, paired with my terrified eyes, keeps them silent. I have let the proverbial elephant out of the bag. It's now tromping all over, all willy-nilly, and I'm freaking out.

And then my dad, Old Faithful, leans in and grips my elbow.

"Well, about time you told me," he says.

I blink. He leans in even further, and the pinch on my elbow now makes all the nerve endings in my hand go numb, but in a good, loving, family-moment sort of way.

"You just saved your life."

TOP TEN WAYS TO TELL YOUR FAMILY
YOU ARE AN ADDICT

1. Don't tell them. In fact, just wait on it for a while. There's no rush. Rushed things are stressful. We don't do stressful anymore, remember? Feel better, then tell them.

2. Do tell them. Go for the right away, "I gotta tell you something" route. Get it off your chest. Feel better afterward.

3. Or, don't feel better. Tell them and realize it was totally not the reaction you wanted, or the right time, or they acted all weird. That's okay, too. This is your stuff, not theirs.

4. Realize that whatever route you choose, it's a visit to the dentist. Not exactly fun. Maybe a bit painful. That's okay. Accept that part.

5. Talk to your friends in your special club. Talk to a counselor. We don't have to run into the dentist's office and shout, "*I'm here! We have to have this appointment right now! It's all drama up in here!*" Dentists don't really need that and neither do you. Get some practice in first.

6. Consider that telling them is not about them anymore. It's about you and your authentic life. It's about boundaries and about protecting your recovery at all costs.

7. If your family drinks, consider that future events might have to bear some repeating on the whole "no I don't drink" thing. You might have to say what you want *out loud* repeatedly. They might need to hear it several

times. This will be annoying, but you could pretend it's a song with a really long chorus. In fact:

8. Apply interpretive dance.

9. With a sequined costume.

10. Or sock puppets. Everything works better with sock puppets. But, eventually, just do it. For you. Not for them.

CHAPTER 15

My Children Are Older
and I Am Not

My three-year-old son is all "big eyes" at me. There is liquid eyeliner festooning my bathroom, in lovely, ebony, cat's-eye scrawls. "Momma, are you mad?" I don't answer. "Like, you are *T-Rex* mad?" Still no response. Henry sighs heavily and mutters, "Wow. T-Rex mad. Dat's mad. And *old."*

I am not old. I am basically a teenager. I learned in recovery that I am now stuck at whatever age I was when I started drinking. I am a forty-five-year-old with a husband, two toddlers, an angry cat, and a rather depressing mortgage. But really? I'm nineteen.

This makes parenting difficult.

Once again I've been hit upside the head with the expectations-versus-reality sledgehammer. My expectations of mothering little ones involved a lot of tasteful Melissa and Doug toys, some Baby Bach twinkling in the background, and a lot of bible verses fluttering about, like they do on Pinterest. My voice would always be an octave below audible but so melodic and soothing that my babies would just *know* what I was communicating to them—like mommy whale speak but slightly less weird. Discipline would be a slight furrowing of the brow paired with demonstrating the correct behavior, all with the patience of Curious George's Man with the Yellow Hat.

Well, I think The Man with the Yellow Hat is on meds.

Reality came swooping in one day after I walked in on a rousing game of Let's Go Potty Decoratively! This game is also a great lesson on gravity, but I didn't go there. Instead, I stared and then asked a really dumb question.

"What are you doing?"

Both boys were silent because they now had to stop and think about what, in the name of hell, they were actually doing. In a toddler's mind, the main answer is, "Who cares? Dis is fun!" but when they looked at my reddened face, they did have the presence of mind to perhaps not answer that way. Thus, they stood there, frozen in their own pee, with guilty smiles and a lot of blinking. They are thinking. And this gives me dead air, which I fill with things like, "What were you *thinking? Really?* You are cleaning this all up! I am *beyond* words! How *could* you?" and other stuff. When I speak this way, it comes across like the "wonk wonk" of the adults in the Peanuts cartoon, but a bit scarier, and my kids tune out.

Playing with pee is not acceptable. But my behavior was not much better, and I supposedly had age and wisdom on my side. The first months of recovery were shocking to me, in their highs and lows, their ebb and flow of hope and peace paired with all the stuffed down feelings of the past twenty years bubbling up at a rapid fire. I relished the moments of calm that told me I was on the right path. I was in the right place. I might even be able to make it through this day without drinking. But then, five minutes later, I would step on a Tinker Toy and hop around in a furious rage, a shouting mess of a mom who could not figure out how to deal with Tinker Toys and recovery at the same time.

I would sit in meetings in a pool of snot and tears. "I'm a terrible mother," I would say. "My kids hate me. I hate me. I yell at them all the time. I don't think . . . " and what I wanted to say was, "I don't see how this is any better than when I was drinking."

There's the rub.

In my attempt to clean up my life and live right, I was living all wrong. Or so it felt at the time.

One morning, I took my boys to a local big-box store. Most shopping excursions lately had been enough to suck the will to live right out of me. So many brightly packaged choices. So many fluorescent lights. So many bra displays. I get overwhelmed. I also get depressed when I see a nightgown that reminds me of one my mom has, and I stop to check the price. It looks comfortable. It would match my sock slippers. And so it goes. It's a slippery slope.

We are about done when I realize I forgot the milk. I sigh and heave the cart to a stop. Both boys are in the cart, getting slowly buried under processed food. One has squished the bread, as is his custom on each store trip. The other is whining. "Canna we have a donut mommy? Please? I am so hunnnnnngggry." The elongating of the word increases the number of glances from fellow shoppers. People are well-versed in whiney children here in big-discount-store land. They like it when other kids whine because, for a moment, it's not their own kid.

Here's what I should have said, "Darling. You had breakfast one hour ago. And it was pancakes with syrup, which, as you know, is not exactly a healthy choice. So, we won't be having sweets again today. We can have some fruit when we get home. Now, attitude of gratitude my sweet prince! Oh look, kale! I'll make you those yummy kale chips you like!"

Instead, I say "Sure, kid."

My theory was simple. I was going to be nineteen for a while, so I was not going to take on parenting *and* sobriety at the same time.

I did realize that exiting the situation entirely would not be the best solution because I was actually still in charge of these tiny humans and pretending otherwise would have gotten me signed up for the loony bin. Or worse. What I did do, instead, was take on the roll of "Fun Mom." We all have a fun auntie, and I learned well from mine. When I was about nine or ten, I visited my Aunt Dorothy in Wichita, Kansas, and all I remember is eating fried ice cream. Oh, and we played miniature golf, and I went a little Tom Watson and hit the ball out of the park and onto a car. But I was with my fun auntie, so there was no yelling!

Since strange and exotic foods hit a real chord with me, I decided this was where we would travel for the next few weeks. As we took our long walk to the back of the store—an arduous trip since the store was as big as a football field—I threw some more boxed macaroni and cheese (orange variety), fruit rollups (no-fruit-in-there variety), and frozen pizza (cardboard variety, but they like them, the weirdos). I also threw in a package of Tin Roof Sundae ice cream. It has nuts. My son can't eat nuts. This would ensure this ice cream would be *all mine*.

When we got home, I'd put on PBS. All the time. I could sing all the songs to Thomas the Tank Engine and Barney. I had a bit of a crush on one of the brothers from the animal adventure show, Wild Kratts, the green-shirted one. Martin Kratt? Or Chris? I don't know. The enthusiastic one. That narrows it down.

We ate a lot of horrible food, and our eyes glazed over as we watched PBS Kids and Little Einsteins videos. Occasionally, I would send them outside to play, or we would head to the library. But for the most part, I was a mom slug. A nineteen-year-old, sugar-riddled, messy-car-driving, preoccupied, and petulant mom who had no clue how to get from one day to the next without alcohol. "Come on boys," I would shout. "Let's go eat cheese fries at the mall!" Translation: the thought of doing laundry and planning dinner makes my detoxed brain fizzle, so I'm going in search of carbs. Come along!

This is recovery at its sloppy best. When alcohol is no longer your beau, the mental processing part of your day slides down to functioning at an amoebic level. I slid around. Sometimes I changed out of my jammies; sometimes I would wash my hair. But when confronted with opening bills or making dinner, my amoeba hands would flair up in despair, and I floated away to some place soft and warm, such as the couch or biggie fries, to wait until I evolved and got more brains.

But I didn't slide over into some gin. I would wistfully reminisce how gin had seemed to help me function at an exceptionally high level. The frenzy of doing would only last for about thirty minutes, but I would pack a lot in those thirty minutes. I *missed* gin. I missed the ice, the crisp taste of pine forests, and the sip that said, "Now everything, *everything*, will be all right."

All I had now were crusty sweatpants and a permanent indent I left in our couch. I should have circled it three times before flopping down on it with a sigh, like Norman used to do. I also had exceptionally bad tantrums. One time I lost my temper at my clothes for being too small and threw a pile in the trashcan with great force, without realizing that our cat, Bob, was asleep in the pile and would likely never speak to me again.

On too many days to count, we headed to McDonalds, where I dipped fries in a shake as my boys ran and yelled in the McDonalds Thunderdome area. "Mommah! Save my fries! I'll be right back!" Charlie would careen by me in his little socked feet, all smiles. I would carefully place his fries and the other nutritionally bereft choices on his tray for him, and we would stay and play the afternoon away. McDonalds had become my healthy choice. It was a hell of a lot healthier there than trying to talk to moms at the park when all I wanted to do that day was cry, or stay home and cry some more, because brushing my teeth and my hair seemed an awful lot to ask. McDonalds was where I could sit and stare at my children, and no one would talk to me. No one would ask how I was, or how teaching was going, or where I had been lately because he or she hadn't seen me at church. No one I knew went to McDonalds nearly as much as I did, so it was safe. It was perfectly safe. When we left for home we all smelled like fries, which is a pleasant perfume when your only joy seems to derive from the heart of darkness inside a deep fryer.

It was all so *not* what I had planned. My mommy skills were up there with those lip-glossed pregnant juveniles on MTV. I guess I should have known. When my boys were infants, I'd been terrible at making sure they had tummy time, so things were pretty much on a downhill slide from the start.

But do you know what? My kids were okay. They were able to hold up their heads fine at three and four years old, so the whole tummy time thing was just a conspiracy to make us buy more parenting books. Their teeth didn't fall out from all the processed food, and if they did, well, they were baby teeth—they were *supposed* to fall out. I know. To be clear, I wasn't keeping the election open for any Mom of the Year awards here.

I was Mom of the Year because I didn't drink. Some nights I'd slide under the covers and sigh so heavily I was sure they could hear it up in Canada, and I thought, *Crap day. Crap mom. Crap dinner. Craptastic. I am a teen mom stuck in the thighs of a forty-four-year-old. All of this is crap.* But then a still, small voice would make one very non-crap point.

But, Dana, you didn't drink today. And that, all by itself, makes you the winner of everything.

TOP TEN WAYS TO WIN AT EVERYTHING

1. Go to meetings and don't drink between meetings. When you fall asleep, thank your Higher Power for simple rules. When you wake up, ask Him for help not to drink today. Simple.

2. Take all your parenting books, the ones with all the lists, healthy suggestions, and great advice, and put them under your bed.

3. When you do that, and you notice the dust bunnies under your bed had sex and made what looks like a dust rhino, ignore it. Dusting is for another day.

4. Watch movies. Get a Netflix subscription. Watch *Gone with the Wind.* Memorize the "I'll do that tomorrow" scene. Watch *FT*. Do the ugly cry. Watch crass, funny, or scary movies. Just keep them coming.

5. Don't worry about your children and television. Give them PBS, and they'll end up smarter than you.

6. Stock up on chocolate, ice cream, Nutter Butters, Blow Pops, and Twizzlers. Hide it. All this is just for you. Also, buy the expensive fizzy San Pellegrino Blood Orange Seltzer even though it costs as much as an orange tree. Allow yourself to understand the irony that one bottle of Pellegrino is a literal drop in the bucket in comparison to all the money you spent on booze.

7. Also buy frozen pizza, mac and cheese, and chicken nuggets that look like dinosaurs. These will be for your children, and your children will be okay. Pizza out of a box is much better than mommy drinking out of a box.

8. Repeat all of the above with abandon. Don't think, *I'll start my diet tomorrow. I'll make kale chips tomorrow.* Let tomorrow take care of itself. If it wants kale chips, take care of it then. Stick with today.

9. Whatever you do, don't think you are failing. You're not. *You're not drinking*, and you are hunkering down. You are doing what you have to do to stay sober. The healthier stuff will come back.

10. Just for today, don't drink.

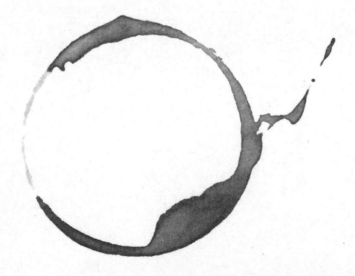

CHAPTER 16

I Find Out I Am No Longer in Control

It is my wedding anniversary. To celebrate, I decide to throw a two-layer carrot cake across the kitchen at my husband.

Sobriety is wobbly. In the bible, the Christian walk is compared to a narrow path that is, at times, difficult or challenging. Recovery takes that path on a detour through one of those terrifying fun houses where all the chairs are on the ceiling and a tilted floor is added for good measure. So when your goal for the day is to make it to a meeting at eight o'clock that night—hopefully with all children fed and watered at that point—sometimes you can get a bit unbalanced.

Or, as my dad would put it, bat-shit crazy.

The biggest challenge I faced in recovery was not cravings, holidays, crying children, or that my cat had decided to pee in the laundry basket again. These external triggers were all swirling around me in a lovely soup of pain that I could pin blame on—as much as you can pin anything on soup. But really, my biggest battle was in my head. My ego's "me-first" voice was loud and had a lot to say. I had listened to it far more than I should have for a very long time.

Here's how an addict's ego works: "I am totally and completely the most important loser in the room!" This confuses others, as you can imagine. It's like trying to take your kid on a pony ride, where the pony alternates between thinking it's at the Preakness and taking a roll in the dust. Either way, your toddler isn't going to be happy. I am that pony. I can't help but imagine that my life, on a daily basis, is so big and important and causes so many vast feelings that I find myself narrating my daily escapades. *Here I am going to get my tires rotated*, I will think. *This is going to be so hard. There are people. They'll ask me questions about tires, and I am not sure how I'll respond. There will be suspenseful waiting as that guy in the overalls stares me down. I think I might cry. And of course, I'll have the boys. They'll probably wander off and fall into one of those well things beneath a car. It could kill them; these auto shops are so unsafe. This really is too much to ask. Why did my husband burden me with this? Today, of all days. Well, really, there's not much going on today, but still. It's hard. It's so hard being me.*

You get the idea. This will later be paired with:

The dude in the coveralls stared at me, and I couldn't come up with the answer quickly enough. I am a horrible, stupid, lowly person. Just a dumb housewife. I bet he will call his wife later and tell her how happy he is that he isn't married to somebody like me. My kids would be better off with a mom who knows the difference between 10W30 and

10W40. What the hell does that mean, anyway? How in the world have I even operated a car all this time without really knowing this? I have no right to breathe air. I bet my husband is going to call this guy later, and they'll commiserate together. He's laughing while he's on his cell. He's talking to Brian right now. I just know it.

It's exhausting. But, I will tell you this. I am really, really good at being this screwed up. Or is that my ego talking?

I dealt with my ego in two paradoxically different ways. My first approach was to ignore all inner voices and stamp them out as quickly as they popped up. This has merit, yes, but it can also create a sort of Sybil reaction in which you end up throwing a carrot cake at your husband.

On my husband's forty-third birthday, I decided to celebrate his geezer status by making his favorite meal—pizza, salad, and homemade carrot cake—which seemed like a good idea at the time. That morning, I started on the cake and the pizza dough and spent the rest of the day in the kitchen, grating carrots and mixing up gloppy cream cheese frosting. Everything was trucking along, and then, well nothing. Nothing happened, really. There was no big, bad, horrible event where someone lost an arm, or we set something on fire, or I accidentally used nutmeg instead of cinnamon in the batter. But at around four o'clock, my head started messing with me.

Thoughts, shriveled and unhappy like stewed prunes, surfaced as I grimly mixed my frosting. *Brian will be home late again, I bet.* Stir. *My arm is getting tired, and this frosting looks just like Elmer's glue. I suck. I should not bake anything again in the history of ever.* Stir, stir. *What is the deal with the lumps? My life is over.* Angry stir. *My kids are yelling. Little savages. Why can't they just get along for longer than four minutes? What is wrong with my family? We are doomed.*

I hate everything. Stir! Stir! Stir!

That night we were going to have a pleasant, loving family meal. Damn it. But little things like toddler wildebeests, a husband who was twenty minutes late, and pizza dough that could have been mistaken for an Amazon box whittled away at those expectations. I began to feel rather peevish.

Actually, I was really ticked off.

We ate dinner as I simmered along, all pruney in my insistence that somehow my husband's birthday dinner had become about me. I parboiled as we ate our salad and fought to chew the pizza dough. My husband, oblivious to it all, opened his presents and cute, garish homemade cards from the boys, while I pruned all over the place.

After the boys were in bed and we were cleaning up in the kitchen, my husband told me, "That was a great meal, honey, thank you." Obviously, he was mocking me. I didn't respond but shut the dishwasher with a bit more force than necessary. And then, he did it. He gave me "the look," the one that sets me off almost as bad as listening to him chew his pizza. He tilted his head to the side like a curious Labrador Retriever and asked the stupidest question in the history of mankind.

"What's wrong?"

The cake is still embedded in the curtains above my kitchen sink. At times, I will be scrubbing something and wonder, what is this stuff? It's like white cement. All splattered like a crime scene with frosting as trace evidence. I've found frosting on the upper cabinets and other random places in my kitchen for years. And each time I found it, I was grateful for my marriage and that Brian's only reaction, after a lot of wide-eyed blinking, was to try and help me clean. By no means was he thrilled—the frosting was slippery and the two of us were skating around on sugar and rage—but he wanted to help. I broke into loud Nancy Kerrigan style sobs that matched, exactly, the dramatic flair of the cake-throwing incident and told him to leave. "Let me clean it up," I said. "Just leave me alone!" And, very wisely, he did.

The arc of that cake, as it traveled over Brian's head, was a beautiful thing. It seemed to float in slow motion before it exploded like a massive snowball of frosting and martyred carrots on the wall. It took two hours to clean it up. The process involved picking up hunks of the sticky stuff, while sobbing, and throwing them into the trash. Then I would slide over to the wall to wipe it down with a rag, really just smearing it on the paint like a poor attempt at modern art. Sobbing all the while.

I really hate carrot cake.

A few months into recovery, Brian and I attended one of our church's potluck suppers after the service. I loved these things. There were Jell-O salads, pastel bowls of other salads that weren't really salads at all, and a gorgeous amount of desserts, a whole table of them, lovingly served by the hostesses of our church. My husband grabbed a heavy slice of carrot cake. The frosting was thick and glossy, almost causing the cake to slide off the paper plate. I nibbled on my lemon bar and watched as Brian shoveled the cake into his mouth with relish. He stopped, aware of being watched, and cocked his head to the side. I steeled myself.

"This is really good. You wanna bite? There's pecans in here!"

I shook my head. "No. It's a symbol."

The head tilted a bit more, and I sighed. It was hard trying to explain deep things to a Labrador Retriever. They were often too happy to bother.

"It's a what?"

"A symbol. It's a symbol of my misplaced anger and rage and how completely wrong I was to throw that cake at you. I had no right, and I have no idea why I did it. So I guess, it's also a metaphor for my struggle, you know. And it's a symbol. It's a symbol and a metaphor. I really, really don't like carrot cake."

"Wow." He eyed the bite on his fork, fraught with so much inner angst and conflict. "I was wrong. It's walnuts, not pecans."

It's a really good thing to be married, if you struggle with ego. Marriage pretty much beats it out of you—as do small children, evil pets, and aging. But, if you are like me and have an extra dose of ego, try my second way of dealing with it. Give your ego an audience only on odd days of the week. The other days, listen for a minute, nod, and then go play Candy Land with your sons. It is important to listen, and then *not* listen, one day at a time. It is a balance, and when I was slowly traversing the wobbly bridge of early recovery, keeping my balance was very difficult.

TOP TEN WAYS TO CHECK YOUR EGO

1. When your eyes open in the morning, ask your Higher Power to help you not use. Say, "Please show me your will and then give me the courage to carry that out."

2. Even if you don't believe in a Higher Power, say it anyway. This is showing great humility and faith. It also feels very weird, but you get used to it.

3. When you lay down at night, say, "Thank you." Your Higher Power knows why, even though you may not, and it's good to say it out loud.

4. Surround yourself with small children and small animals. They need you to feed them. Ego can't really mess with that.

5. Don't ask questions if you don't want to know the answers.

6. Consider saying no once in a while. Don't volunteer out of obligation or guilt; this will only lead to resentment. Volunteering and seething resentment don't go well together.

7. However, help people. Think outside the box. Be available. Try to understand boundaries and selflessness. These two *do* go together. It's a dance.

8. Be patient. Mastering helping people is hard.

9. When in doubt, remember who you are: greatly loved. This doesn't mean you have to be great; you just have to really sit with the love part.

10. Have a four o'clock '80s dance party in your living room. Do this every day. Schedule it on your phone if you have to. Your ego will thank you for the boogie. And you can't take yourself too seriously while slow dancing with your toddler to Spandau Ballet.

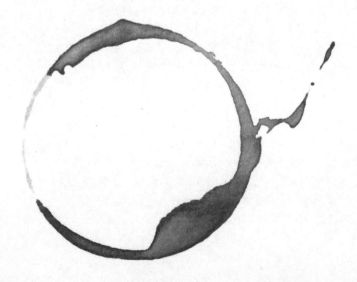

CHAPTER 17

Christopher Scott

I am eleven, and it's taco night at our house. This is important because it's the one night we all gather together in mutual love of tacos, and the fact that my mom is never stingy with the grated cheese. My mom revolves around the table like a satellite, never sitting down to eat until we are almost done, it seems. That's her thing.

My brother is quoting *The Blues Brothers*. He is acting out the entire movie, practically word for word, inserting sound effects and a musical number here or there. He does a great Aretha Franklin. He does a great John Belushi.

My brother is our John Belushi. He is irreverent and contagiously fun. He has us laughing so hard around the dinner table we are teary eyed. When my sister and I are washing the dishes, Chris waits until my hands are deep in the hot, sudsy water. He grabs me in his famous, semi-paralyzing neck hold and bellows at both of us, "We are on a mission from God," and we squeal. He gives me a noogie that makes my eyes smart, and then he is gone. He disappears into his room only to re-emerge in a waft of Brut and a skin-tight polyester shirt, transformed into a young John Travolta, on his way to the local nightclub, Bananas, to dance.

My brother would practice intricate dance routines with my older sister, Sherry, in the living room. They had on the soundtrack to *Saturday Night Fever*, of course. They kept changing the song for their routine, but I hoped they'd pick *Stayin' Alive.* It was my favorite. Sherry had long, brown hair, which she curled with hot rollers to create a perfect Farrah Fawcett wave. Chris wore a gold chain and tight, white pants. I was sure I'd never seen anything so glamorous as I sat on the couch, mute in reverence, watching them concoct six different ways to hustle. Bananas, their favorite disco, was having a dance contest, and Chris wanted to win. I knew he could.

Chris could do anything. He was, in my mind, starting quarterback, most popular, most likely to succeed, and most likely to be the coolest brother ever. Sometimes I would sneak into his room while he was away at practice or out with his friends. The room was a mess, but I would tiptoe about like I had entered some sort of shrine to coolness with scattered jerseys and a baseball mitt on the floor. In the closet, I would pull at the sleeve of his letterman jacket (rarely there as he wore it constantly). It smelled like leather and promise. His dresser was the best find, displaying his relics of manhood—keys, coins, stray bits of paper with mysterious phone numbers and ciphers of romance, and, sometimes, homework. I pored over the books, squinting at his illegible scrawl for clues to his smarts and abilities. The top drawer always had a huge bag of Raisinets or peanut M&Ms in it. I'd sneak a handful and would chew as I reflected and searched through Chris's things and hoped to find him.

My brother was nearly eight years older than me. Sherry and Chris were my half siblings, part of our family by my dad's first marriage. Half sibling sounded to me like some sort of truncation, like they didn't really count or measure up somehow, which was *not* how I regarded Sherry and Chris. Chris lived with his mom for years, but he came to live with us when he was a teenager, and I was simply delighted. Up until that point, it had been just me and my sister Jenni, and I was excited—my brother was coming! He was like a celebrity. I told everyone, "My brother is gonna come live with us. He's in high school. He looks like Richard Gere." Most of my friends didn't know who that was, so I would add with an air of superiority, "You know, *American Gigolo?* He is cute like that." The movie was clearly beyond my viewing years, so I had sneaked it, I think, while babysitting. Thank you, HBO. At any rate, comparing my brother to a male prostitute didn't seem like a poor choice to me, but I am pretty sure Chris would not have been pleased.

My brother had friends. They were big, tall ones that were kind of blended together in appearance. Quite a few of them were named Dave. They smelled of Brut, or maybe something else a bit sweeter, and they took up the space in our house, all arms and legs and big laughter. They would go downstairs to his room and listen to his Steve Martin record or the Steve Miller Band. For the longest time, I thought one of his friends was actually Steve Miller, but later after some asking and embarrassment, I realized the name was common. It seemed totally possible for my cool brother to be hanging out with the lead singer of a famous band.

Chris's friends didn't actually come over that often. I only have a few memories of the dancing. Memories of those times are filed carefully, and when I take them out, I make sure they are put back in their placeholder—My Big Brother. I have a picture my mom gave me of Chris heading to prom. He's wearing a white tuxedo with big lapels and has fluffy brown hair. He is looking down at me, and I am looking up at him. I hope he is saying something to me, something funny and kind. He's probably telling me to not touch his car, but even so, he is smiling at me. The sun is setting. To me, any time he would stop and smile or throw a comment my way was golden.

There were some memories that weren't so golden. One morning we were piling in the car to leave for Grandma's house. Chris was still asleep downstairs. As we loaded up our packed picnic lunch, Mom noticed that somehow, rather tragically, all the desserts were missing. She had splurged, you see, on highly processed, packaged desserts of the Twinkie variety for our lunches. This was a big deal. The crinkly paper and that cream interior were heaven. In those days, there were two types of kids unpacking their lunch boxes at school: the pudding cup kids and the homemade oatmeal cookie kids. We were the homemade kids, and I would have sold my leg warmers for one tin can with the sharp pull-off lid of chemical-laden chocolate goodness. For some reason, Mom had taken pity and finally provided us with some of the good stuff for our long day at Grandma's. I do now see a direct correlation between visiting family and the need for special sugar treats. It was simply heartbreaking. I had known about that Twinkie for twenty-four hours and was so excited I'd grabbed my own paper bag lunch and gleefully peeked, probably thinking, *Soon, my pretty,* as I looked inside—but no Twinkie.

Chris had come home late the night before. In a fit of the munchies, he had opened our lunches and eaten just the desserts. It was as if the Grinch stole Christmas morning right out from under us. Mom stared at her hands and then said, "Go back. I need to talk to him." And my dad did. He drove right back to our house, and we all sat in the car while Mom went inside and, I am pretty sure, made her feelings quite clear.

I recall this because my mom didn't usually fuss with Chris. She adored him like we all did, but he was a stepson, and she didn't want to step over the line; perhaps she thought he had a halfway mark where she could only discipline him so much and then she had to back off. But the Twinkies were the final, sugary straw.

Chris had been having some problems with school, drinking, and getting in trouble. He fought a lot with my dad. He didn't talk much to us anymore and seemed stuck in the sullen teenager mood.

All I wanted was to hear him impersonate John Belushi and maybe call me "Brainabus" again, his pet name for me. I didn't understand the problems that were stewing. I just wanted a brother.

Chris eventually moved back in with his mom, and I missed him, sort of. We saw him on the weekends.

And then, we all grew up. We left for college and jobs and to experience life. We grew apart. We saw each other on holidays. One time Chris came to our family farm for a get-together, and we fished. He told me where to cast. I leaned into his shadow and his words, drinking up the moments I had with him.

He got married. His wife, Lynn, was so sweet and fun, and we rejoiced. Lynn would be our gateway to Chris, an outstretched hand that would help us on board. He wasn't distant, as much as he was busy, it seemed.

He got divorced. He drank too much, and then Lynn was gone. I saw him about once a year, at Thanksgiving. When we saw each other he'd give me those big hugs, the ones that threatened to squeeze the air out of me. He swore he would have us over, as soon as the house was fixed up. He would have us over for dinner, some time soon, as soon as he did whatever else he needed to do to his flooring, his walls, his bathrooms, and his life.

He slowly took the doors on his world and shut them tight against me. And I never tried to open them. I sent a birthday card once in a while. Once, in my thirties, I called him for help after a breakup from my boyfriend of seven years. I had gone to a doctor's appointment and was scared to death after the doctor told me, "You are drinking every night; this is dangerous behavior. You might need to go into rehab." I was terrified and called Chris. We didn't talk much, and it seemed weird to even dial his number. But he came and talked to me, told me to do the right thing. He told me he knew what it was like to suffer from addiction. "That stuff, it will mess you up," he said. "But, I don't think you need inpatient care or anything. I just think you need to go to church. Get some good friends. It'll be okay, Dana." It was the most we had talked in ages. I think back on that now and wonder, what if I had gone? Would I have listened then?

The last time I talked to Chris, he was newly sober after an especially bad drinking binge. Outpatient rehab was on the table. Losing his job and possibly losing his house were on the table. He was attending meetings on a daily basis. He was trying. When I saw him, I was shocked. He had lost so much weight his jeans drooped off of him almost comically. He had a shifting gaze and was constantly fidgeting. Psoriasis plagued him, and sleeping became difficult because he was uncomfortable. He pulled at his shirt and fidgeted with his sleeves. He seemed so utterly uncomfortable with himself, with us, with sitting and talking. His eyes would not meet mine. I leaned in for a hug, but this time it was me who clung to him. He just seemed to wait for the hugs to end.

I hoped for him to play with my boys; Chris always loved kids and was the fun uncle to my nephews. But Charlie and Henry, even in their toddler cuteness, did not seem to interest him. I positioned them close to him to see if it would make him smile or spark a funny comment, but he was distracted. And just unhappy.

The Chris who had given us a perfect impersonation of John Belushi was gone.

And in a few months' time, Chris would be gone for good.

He had liver damage, and it was working its way to fatality. He didn't stay sober much longer after Thanksgiving. Dad begged him, one more time, to get sober—but to no avail. Chris lost his job and disappeared. Occasionally we would get texts from him, mostly unintelligible. One said, "You are the best sister I ever had." I wondered, *How? How so?* I couldn't help him and was barely a part of his life, mostly just watching from afar like I were gazing at a painting, critiquing it. When I was drinking,

I had a lot of opinions about Chris—how he needed to stop drinking and get into rehab; how he needed no enabling or coddling; and how he was just a mess.

During that last Thanksgiving, I had fewer opinions. I'd been going to meetings for several months and had over a year in recovery. I had no more opinions on what he should do.

I had shyly approached him out on the back patio, and spoken with him about my own battle. We both faced out to the yard, gripping onto our Diet Cokes and watching my boys play soccer. He had listened quietly, and told me, "Well, that's good. That's good, Dana. Good for you," but he never looked at me. I felt like I was trying to talk to his heart, and he wanted to look past the conversation, and the words. It was almost like he didn't believe me and thought there was no way I was part of his special club. And the moment, when we talked on that back patio, seemed so disconnected in outcome, like watching airplane exhaust trails crisscross in the sky heading in completely different directions.

I only wanted to talk to him. And it did no damn good. He still died in the end.

The last time I saw Chris, he was no longer able to speak. His girlfriend had called my dad and told him that Chris had been taken by ambulance to the hospital. Chris was released to hospice within days. When I saw him, I sat by his side and lay my head on his chest to listen to his heart. It was too late.

Chris's body was swollen and bruised from acute liver failure. His skin was yellow. He had doses of morphine administered regularly, and we sat with him and waited.

We waited for my handsome, funny, charming brother to die.

The evening after Chris's funeral, we came home to my father-in-law's house. I climbed the stairs to our upstairs guest room and sat on the bed, a lump of exhaustion. Even crying was too hard. I stared at a wall and then at the flower arrangement and the drapes. *Wow*, I thought, *Ed really did this room up nice. He has a nice color scheme going here.* I then wondered at my wonderment. How would I do this? This whole pain thing did not sit right with me. I had a tenacious grip on minutia, on the countless tasks and plans of a mom of two little ones; but now, every few minutes or so, a horrifying snag at my heart would leave me breathless and sick.

He's gone. I will never be able to talk to him again. And my heart would break.

The ebb and flow of this was uncomfortable. And this I found unacceptable. So, as is my first reaction to any sort of malaise or uneasiness, I thought about drinking.

Only this time, I was aware of a crucial point of interest: I was at my father-in-law's house. My father-in-law was a social drinker. My father-in-law had booze in this house, right now. And I was alone. My family had left to get dinner, and I had said I wanted to stay home, take a bath, and head to bed.

I could go drink, and no one would know.

I walked downstairs to the kitchen, opened the freezer, knew right where to find it: the gin bottle, pretty and cold. Waiting. I stared at it; we said our hellos; and I shut the door. I then walked over to the garage door, heading out to the refrigerator that held the good stuff—margarita in a bottle, wine, and beer. I stared as if it were a fireplace, and I was tired. So tired.

"Hello, alcohol. It's been a while. Did you know my brother died today? Well, he did. I said the eulogy. I feel like I want to cry right now but staring at you is helping." I shut the door. I could taste the wine so much my lips tickled. I felt the pucker of the margarita. I knew the gin would burn but then follow with a delightful cool slide into numb. I opened the door again, felt the cold air on my face, and stared.

"So, how are you? It's me again. Oh, there's some Bailey's. Now that's a delightful little drink. My best friend in college loves that stuff. She likes it over ice cream. I always thought that was a waste of time. Ice cream just gets in the way." I blinked and sighed, suddenly so homesick for Bethany, my friend from college, who loved a glass of Bailey's once in a while and who asked me, once, "Why are you drinking alone? Why, Dana?" If she were here she would give me a hug, and I would cry, like a normal person, instead of standing here conversing with booze.

"So, I think I better go now. And, well . . . don't take this personally. But you can suck it."

I slammed the door so hard the bottles all clinked noisily inside. I trudged upstairs. I took a bath. And sobbed. Sober.

TOP TEN WAYS TO STAY SOBER THROUGH REALLY HARD STUFF

1. Get community. Get into meetings. Get a counselor. Get a sponsor. Get a church. Get close to those who have been there and can listen.

2. Get the phone. Dial numbers. Get used to calling people even when you think it's going to be a pain for them, annoy them, or interrupt them. Ignore that voice. Have a group of numbers to call when you need to.

3. Get a move on. Get up and out the door. Get some fresh air. Go for a walk, every day, and talk to God.

4. Get really mad at your Higher Power. It's okay. It isn't fair.

5. Get a grip. At times it's important to remember how strong you are and how far you have come.

6. Put on your thinking cap. Think through the drink. Think about how it will be after one and what will happen after two. Think about how you can't handle even one sip anymore and how you will feel tomorrow morning when you wake up with a terrible headache and an aching heart. Think it through. All the way through. Talk it out, even out loud, if you have to. You know where it will go.

7. Get used to it. Pain will happen. Bad things will, too. We are not so special that we cornered the market on sadness.

8. Get your arsenal ready. Have a plan. Know the triggers. Know what helps. Surround yourself with these things. I keep a Big Book in my car, by my bed, and on my phone. I allow myself chocolate and ice cream and any other sugar bomb I want, whenever I need them. I repeat the Serenity Prayer like it's some magical mantra, and it is. It distracts and softens the heart.

9. Get honest. Really honest. How much will drinking through this hurt those around you? How much will it hurt you? Get humble. Realize, also, as much as this hurts, that you are getting stronger with each breath and with each tear in your heart. Stronger.

10. Get on your knees and pray.

CHAPTER 18

The Big Tell, Part Three

At some point, I am going to have to sit down and have "the talk" with my sons. Not the sex talk. That's up to Brian. My discussion will be about booze and how to avoid it at all costs, or I will kill them.

Charlie started kindergarten. This is completely impossible. But yet, we took him, gigantic backpack and Spiderman lunchbox and all, and they actually had a seat for him inside and said it was true; he was enrolled. It was time. On his first day, I walked him to school and held Brian's hand as our two sons ran ahead, scattering and darting about like bad drivers. It's all a race to them. They race to finish their Cheerios first, to body slam the cat before the other one does, and to be the most slobbery after brushing their teeth. We've watched *Cars* seven thousand times. This movie, along with a toddler's natural penchant for being the best at anything he can, even about who has the highest arc and velocity when pottying, has made our household a highly competitive arena.

As we walk to the school, I just want to slow down. I watch him, his backpack the size of a Volkswagen, as he shouts and bursts into a run again. He almost trips over the brick sidewalk, and I reach out my hand, but I'm half a block away. I don't have those super powers. If he falls, he falls; I would only be able to run and hold him afterward. Realizing this is one of those mom lessons we have to deal with on a daily basis as our young ones grow up. We can only put on Band-Aids. We can listen but can't stop painful things. We can't go to the playground and beat up the bully. We can't take back the words that tell him he's a poophead. We can only apply pressure, and a hug, and listen—after the fact.

I hate it. I hate that I can't hover around him like an over-protective honeybee. And I also hate it that my tendencies toward hovering makes me one of those neurotic helicopter moms I used to complain about in the staff room. So I take a breath, squeeze Brian's hand, and pray that we make it to the school without tears. My tears.

The drinking thing took my mommy heart and broke it open. It's still healing, and in that process, I decided my children should never have to suffer any pain again. They had to deal with a drunk mom in their babyhood, and it's up to me to make it up to them now.

I know; this is totally stupid.

As one who used to hide wine bottles in her boots in the closet, I now understand that reality and I were not friends. We still have issues, reality and me. We are working through them. I go to therapy and meetings and work on it, and reality just keeps on . . . being. It sucks because it feels like I have so much more work to do. Reality is such a pain in the ass.

At any rate, reality is now calling on me to talk to my kids about my alcoholism. Charlie is six years old and has the cognitive skills of a "pre-med who hasn't picked a college yet" kid. Henry is four, and so we have him at the "going to take the ACT next month" level. They come home from school and preschool and work on quadratic equations for fun while I make dinner. In other words, briefing them on the cold hard facts about addiction should be no problem.

This, I know, is also totally stupid.

As is my tendency, I find myself playing the lovely game of "It's All or Nothing!" with emotional decisions. Either I lay it all out with my boys and give them the whole sordid story, or I tell them I'm leaving for crocheting class every Monday and Wednesday night (sometimes Sunday, too, if it's been quite the week). All this teeter-totter behavior has me rather dizzy. And I heard somewhere how children might not thrive on waffling and inconsistency as the main parenting style from their mother. It says so in one of those parenting books I pulled out from under the bed.

It was time to get a plan.

First of all, I talked to my sponsor. Getting a sponsor is this thing we meeting people do. It's like hiring someone to watch your every move and talk to you on a daily basis, even if you don't want the person there. Also, the sponsor insists, at least with me, that I am not a bother, but, deep down, I wonder if she sighs heavily before she answers my calls. She does answer, and I talk; then she listens and gives advice. Often she just lets me work it out and gives me a hug over the phone in the form of a low chuckle. I can hear her smile at me, and it helps. She gets me. She tells me, "Just tell them what they need to know. The sick, sad past is not really necessary. They might not really need to get all the information, Dana." She's right, of course. With younger ones, the goal would be simply to answer their questions and give them the most direct and pertinent low-down, for their sake and yours.

At the dinner table that night, I clean up a bit early. It is interesting. I find myself in the same satellite behavior now as my mom, always hovering, never really sitting down to dinner. At some point, I remind Charlie to take his medicine tonight before bed, and then tell him, "I'm going to a meeting. I'll be back to give you kisses." He has little protest, and neither does Henry. They are more interested in building mashed potato sculptures. I wonder if I need to have the talk with them, so I look over at Brian. My eyes ask the question. He smiles and shakes his head. I am to wait for the questions. I am fine.

And I go. And at some point later, when we're in the car and heading home as dusk gathers, Charlie asks, "Do I get to wrestle tonight, Momma?" I nod yes.

Henry asks, "You comin'?" And I shake my head no. "Why?"

"Tonight is my meeting, remember? I am going to a meeting, but I'll be home after you get back from practice to give you hugs and kisses."

Silence from the backseat. Then, "Why?"

I know he's not asking why the hugs and kisses. I know it. So I take a breath and say, "Mommy goes to meetings to learn how to be a better mommy." I wait a minute. "The meetings, they are full of people like me, who had some bad habits and who need to talk to others to get better."

"Whassa 'bad habit'?" I am not at all sure if this is going to go where I want. I am not at all sure if this is how I'm supposed to do this. I pray for a minute because that's what my sponsor told me. When in doubt, don't rush. Pray. Just wait. Be still. Keep your mind on the Serenity Prayer. Keep your mind on remembering your turn signal. Keep your mind on the fact that this is not going to kill you, you talking to them. You don't need to make it a big thing.

I explain, very simply, that sometimes we turn to things that make us feel better, if only for a little while. Like how we can find ourselves watching television all day because we're bored or tired. Then when we get up, we're all cranky and lost, kind of, on how to go about our day. Both boys nod solemnly. "When we do that, sometimes we find ourselves wanting to watch more and more, because we have gotten into the habit. And those bad habits are hard. Remember when you ate a bunch of candy at church that day? And you ate more than you should have?"

"Yep."

"And what did your tummy feel like?" Charlie and Henry look at each other and grin.

"Pretty bad." More grinning.

"Well, that was me. I kept trying to do the same thing, over and over, because I was kind of stuck and wanted to feel better. But, just like with the candy, it only made me feel sick. And I needed help to stop it, so that's why I go to meetings."

"But what did you eat? Der candy?"

And so here we are. I have to say it. "I drank something called wine. A lot of it. It's also called alcohol. It is not good for me."

All is quiet from the backseat. I left it at that. They didn't ask much more, and we had arrived home. I prayed all the while as we walked into the house, as we greeted the cat. I have no idea if I should have said more, or less. But that's what I said. And if I know anything, I trust my Higher Power, if it's covered in prayer, to take care of the rest.

There is so much more to tell them. But not yet.

When my brother died, and we all walked through the misery of it, questions were asked. I told them he died because his liver stopped working. I told them he was sick. That's it. I tried to tell them more, but each time I did my throat would close. I wondered, sometimes, if my God was gently placing His hand on my head, telling me, "Peace to you, child. It's okay. Save this conversation for later."

And so I will. But as my children and I grow older, I will converse with them about this in other ways. When my son and I walked, hand in hand, to his school, I was present. I was real. I was not in a fog of headachy remorse and sadness. As we go to our first T-ball games or our first Christmas pageants, I will be in the seats, sitting and watching my boys in their cute glory—not anxiously thinking about when I can get home and get away from all the noise and people and into a glass of red. *That* is the conversation, for now, and it is more than enough. And so is my joy. My joy is for their homeruns and their sweet, earnest faces as they sing "Away in a Manger," but also for me, that I am here, alive and *present*, to share these days with them. As each child grows, I find my conversations with them changing as I go to meetings and carry on with being in recovery at all costs.

When will I know to tell them more? My sponsor tells me to listen to my boys. They will tell me when they need to know more. They might not say it directly. I am pretty sure Henry isn't going to come crawling up in my lap one day and say, "Mommy tell me the story about how you stopped being drunk all da time. We love that one." I know. But in their own way, they will tell me. I think the key will be to be in their lives, without circling madly around them, and to be aware.

I realize this all sounds really hard. It kind of makes me want to drink, all this not drinking and then talking or not talking about it.

But I won't. Because, well, one day I would have to talk about that, too. And one big tell to my boys will be enough. That big tell will be going on for the rest of our lives together, as I walk through recovery, and they walk along with me. They don't call it a family disease for nothing. We're all in this together.

TOP TEN WAYS TO TALK TO YOUR KIDS ABOUT YOUR RECOVERY

1. Do not panic. All does not need to be revealed in one huge big momentous talk. This is not *Sweeney Todd*. It's life.

2. Do not avoid. That's like realizing there is a bit of Sweeney in your life and wanting it, so badly, to just be Barney all the time. Rated R movies with voice-overs changing all the profanity to "Mother Sugar" don't work either.

3. If your math teacher gave you a quiz and you answered all the questions and then made up a bunch more questions and answered them too, he would think you're crazy. Just stick with the questions you get.

4. Pray. A lot. Any time your Higher Power prods you, get real and talk a bit. Wait until you're in the car. That way there's no eye contact, and the children are contained.

5. Understand that, as your children grow older, they might deserve more information. They are little humans, after all. Dumbing it all down when they're not so dumb isn't respectful.

6. Consider sock puppets.

7. Just kidding, the kids are probably way past puppet shows. Maybe get some help from outside sources. There are numerous resources and family counselors to help with this. You're not on your own. You're never on your own here.

8. If you decide to add copious ladles full of mom guilt and tears to this, you're probably not going to get the best results. You can put frosting on grovel cake, but it's still going to taste like crap.

9. Recovery is a daily choice. Keep this in mind. That's the biggest conversation you will ever have with your kids.

10. Love yourself. Listen to yourself. You love and listen to your family, so *do the same for you*.

CHAPTER 19

Steve the Sobriety Cat

I am wondering if making amends to my sons while they are sleeping is what the Big Book had in mind.

It had been a particularly difficult day. It started with a sad event at the park involving a slide and some pants that ripped. I had been talking with my friend Rae, taking in the sun, the moment of peace, and fresh air. I felt like a good mom. *Here we are at the park*, I'm thinking. *This is what normal moms do.* Actually, this is what *good* moms do. I feel light, like the sunny air, and wonder if I should try to push the odds and serve my boys some kale at lunch. Then, I hear it, the loud pulsing wail of a kid who is really hurt, not fake hurt or mad. We moms, even the mediocre ones, know the difference on this.

I run to the slide and spot Henry, huddled at the bottom with a bloody lip and scraped chin. He tries to explain, as he does, with each bump or bruise. This would be helpful, as understanding the injury is always good when first aid is needed, but Henry's explanations always come out like this: "IWASSAONDASLIDEANDERWASDAGIRLANDSHEPUSHEDDDDDDDERWASBOOMICANNAHOLDONNNNOUCHMOMMAOUCH! OUCH! OUCH! OUCHIEEEEEEEE!"

It's difficult to work with this, mainly because he is trying to climb up me with snot all over while maintaining the wailing at ninety decibels or more. I try to wipe tears and figure out if there are broken limbs, but the child has turned into a puddle of hurt. I just hug him. He takes the wailing up a notch, and my right ear is now deaf, but it's all I can do.

Moms surround me. Wipes and Band-Aids are offered. My friend Alissa is a walking medevac of ointment, gummy bears, and Kleenex. And that's when it starts. My "Why can't you be normal?" voice shows up. I hate her.

This voice is not, I hope, some sign of deeper, more Sybil-like problems, but she complains a lot to me. She tells me many things, like I should be completely well by now, that I might be able to drink now, that just possibly this whole addiction thing is bogus, and I deserve some tequila tonight. She also tells me I'm fat, and I need to lose twenty pounds—by the end of the week. It doesn't matter that the only way to do so would be to lop off a limb; she is not one for medical common sense. She also tells me I'm fat because I eat too many frozen Snicker bars at night when I'm craving something to give me a sugar high, when all I really need is a good slug of vodka. Then I'd be skinny *and* drunk. Total bonus. She says, of course, that my parenting is *mediocre* at best because she really knows how I hate that word.

She tells me normal people can handle it. Normal people have it together. Normal people don't find large groups so befuddling that even Sundays are tough because church is so full of people. Good, Christian people, sure, but they're all over the place. She tells me, "Why do church? And in fact, why do meetings? Why do anything outside at all? It's too hard. You can't handle it. Why can't you just be normal?"

"Drink up," she says.

But then, "You are a spineless mess for wanting to drink at all. How could you?"

All this bitchiness from her just makes me want to drink all the more, of course. If we fall apart in our self-loathing and recrimination, it just makes it all the easier to fall into a big drink. It's the old story of the insecure chicken and the egg.

That voice starts in, and I have a lot of options.

Option A is to simply listen to her. The tramp. This makes the rest of the day follow a predictable path of anger and depression to what psychiatrists love to call a "self-fulfilling prophecy," but what I prefer to call "I hate my horrible life craptasticness."

Option B is tantrum up. Stomp around. Yell. Rage against the machine and all that.

Option C is to try to do one thing differently. I could pray, journal, or call my ever-patient sponsor and leave a five-minute message. I could sit with the Serenity Prayer for a while. I could try and stand on my head. Rae is nearby; she's also my yoga instructor, so I'm sure she'd help.

Problem is, Option A and B are so much easier.

The rest of the day I felt myself sinking slowly into despair. I'd been sober for almost a year now. I attended meetings at least twice a week. I worked the Twelve Steps; this means a lot of different things to different people, but to my sponsor and me it meant a lot of journaling, thinking, and talking about what was, how I have changed, and how I am now. I woke up and said, "Please," and went to bed at night with a "Thank you." I was walking along, clean and sober.

And damn it all if I didn't still have days where I felt so anxious, and unable to be normal, that the top of my head might fly off if I got a paper cut.

Why do alcoholics drink and addicts use? Many reasons. Paper cuts. Large churches packed full of talkative people. Toddlers who communicate with the drama of German opera, minus the costumes.

We drink or use because we want to control; we need to organize our world, our brains, and our small children. When that becomes difficult, we fuss. And then we feel guilty about fussing, overly so, therefore, we drink. We then feel guilty (rightly so) about drinking, so we drink some more to help that out. We drink because our dad and our brother did, and if we take the time to investigate, pretty much everyone else in the family did, which is disturbing, but also freeing in a sick sort of way.

Sometimes we drink because we are so happy and at peace, suddenly, that we don't know what to do about it but smush it. If we are happy, that means we *won't* be happy soon, and that is awful. We drink because being a grown-up sucks. Sometimes we drink for no other reason than we are bored, and it's all we've done for ages, so why change now?

We drink and use for a lot of reasons. But mainly, we drink and use because we're alcoholics and addicts.

The day had been horrible. I had flailed around with it so badly that when bedtime came even the children were relieved. We all gratefully skulked off to our separate corners, and as I lay there under the covers, feeling hot tears course down my face and staring at the ceiling, I had the classic moment that teeters so very close to relapse: *I am the worst mom in the history of moms. Anything has got to be better than this.*

Recovery has a funny way of not being great sometimes. Neither, it seems, is life in general. But I don't care about the generalizations. I am interested in what I'm feeling, and that night I was feeling a lot like a big bucket of crud. Recovery is hard. It's relentless. But a small voice came to me as I lay there, pondering how bitter it all was: "If you drank again you'd feel a blessed, cool numb for all of ten minutes. But then, the bitterness would only return, this time paired with a lot more sadness than you can even fathom right now."

At that point, as I was almost convulsing with self-loathing, my cat, Bob, jumped up on the bed. Bob is a small, gray Siamese mix. It is also good to point out, for her sake, that Bob is a female with a bobbed tail. We don't know how the tail got that way, and she, I am sure, doesn't know how she got stuck with a male name. She is also slightly cross-eyed and extremely tense. She is quite the pet. Bob has no clue about self-promotion, so she has latched on to the other non-normal being in the house as her only friend. She comes out at night, a little vampire kitty with a goofy cross-eyed look and some trust issues, and flings herself at me in a furry codependent frenzy of "pet me, pet me, pet me" behavior that is cute, but a bit overwhelming. Her favorite game is to stand on my stomach with her pathetic stub of a tail at salute, in my face, pondering for what seems like hours where she should curl up. The cat has no pride. In short, she is completely messed up, and I love her. Bob was a gift from a friend who attends the meetings I go to, and I find this perfectly fitting. Bob is in recovery, too, it seems. She has a ways to go, but one day, around the time the boys are leaving the house to go off to college, she might let them give her a pat.

One day, when Henry spotted her slinking around the steps and flung himself at her with optimism, Bob was so startled she sprang straight up, not out. Gravity won out, and poor Henry suffered a large scratch because of it. Bob nearly had a heart attack. Even her fur was tense after that for quite a while. Henry sobbed pitifully, "Why can't we get a kitty that we canna pet, Mommy? Bob is *cross*."

That night, as I cried and cuddled Bob with mutual screwed-up codependency, I realized what I needed to do. Why had I not thought of this before?

Let's get a kitty!

This is brilliant. I can't drink, and I have the moral character of the Grinch at times, therefore, I am desperate for a change. I've learned in my meetings to change one thing, just one thing, if life doesn't seem to be running smoothly, so I will use a tactic I haven't tried yet at all. Buying my children's love should really work, right?

It doesn't work that way, but that's not the point.

Steve is what we got. Steve is a huge, white and yellow cat who has the personality of Spicoli from *Fast Times at Ridgemont High*.

My children carry him around with his paws lolling about, his fat, furry belly hanging out, and his placid eyes checking out the scene. He never gets mad. He loves to cuddle. He spoons with the boys. He spoons with me. When he purrs it is so deep and loud it sort of sounds like the train sound on our noise machine. It's a deep rumble, and it's adorable. Steve doesn't seem to mind that his paws hardly seem to hit the ground on a daily basis. He is constantly being flattened, smushed, carted, boxed up in the laundry baskets, heaved, hefted, and, once, folded by my boys. He just purrs along, his furry face never quite losing its air of resigned love and mellowness. I love this cat. When we get home, he bounds up like a dog, places his paws on Charlie's shoulders, and head-butts him. I once found him grooming Charlie behind his ears. It was weird, but Steve just raised his furry eyebrow like, "He is my human. It's cool." The cat has, I am convinced, a serious stash of catnip somewhere in my house, but I don't mind. At least somebody in this house gets to have a buzz.

Steve was one of those straight-up gifts from God. He was an impractical one, as my husband likes to point out when we find ourselves in awe of our kitty litter purchases over a month. I don't care, though. I think my sweet Lord took pity on me and said, "Methinks I shall sendeth her this fair cat that is basically an angel with fur," and we are grateful. I don't know why I think God speaks in Elizabethan English, but it just fits. It's sort of like how I expect Steve to speak like a surfer with a lot of "Dude, chill out. Let's sit here and watch ourselves some *Antiques Roadshow*. You down? I'll purr and look all cute and furry."

I'd heard of ESAs (Emotional Support Animals), but I'd never really taken the concept seriously. By now, if I could get away with it, I would strap a little blue vest with some sort of official medical patch on my Steve and cart him around everywhere I go. We could take him with us to the Super Time-Suck Center. If I found the fluorescent lights and the fact that organic grapes cost more than a nice pair of jeans too overwhelming, I could just bury my face in his fury chest and breathe. Steve smells like a mix of wooly cat and gingerbread—I'm not kidding. Really, that is all I need in this life when the chips are down: a fluffy, nutmeggy cat.

Even Bob has embraced Steve. Steve must emit a haze of mellow because Bob has serious love for the white cat. I have walked in on them both, tussling on our bed, and have actually said, "Oh, I'm sorry," and ducked out, all embarrassed. They are both fixed, mind you, but their love is *real*.

One morning I got an email from *The Huffington Post* about an article I had written. Was I willing to be interviewed by some twenty-year-old hipster on *Huffington Post Live,* in about an hour? About my alcoholism? For a lot of people to see? The interesting point here is that *Huffington Post Live* is called that because it is very, *very* live.

I had an hour to figure out how to be calm about this. The problem was what in the world was I going to do with my hair. At one point, after quite a bit of teasing and hair spray, I stared in the mirror and marveled, *This is wonderful. And awful. I am now the famous alcoholic-in-recovery mom. And my hair looks like a brown football helmet, like Sally Fields in* Steel Magnolias. As I sat and waited, nervously fixing my collar and wondering if I should throw up now or afterward, Steve sauntered up. He curled up at my feet for the duration of the entire interview. At one point he actually extended his warm paw and placed it on my foot as if to say, "Dude. Chillax. You're helping people, man. And brah, that's golden."

Whenever I cycle into a bad place in my head, I find Steve. We sit still. Steve isn't one for rushing around. We cuddle. He licks his paws, and I watch in adoration. At times Brian has walked in on the two of us and smirked, "Do I need to leave you two alone?" I just clutch Steve up under my chin and glare.

"You clearly do not understand our love! We have a bond. This is spiritual, dude."

Brian rolls his eyes a bit. "Obviously Steve has been wearing off on you a bit."

There are worse things.

TOP TEN WAYS TO TREAT YOURSELF BECAUSE RECOVERY IS HARD

1. Figure out what you like to do. This could take some time. You haven't really understood yourself in a long while. Dabble in things. Pick up hobbies, Quit them. Don't finish things. Find new things. Write ideas on brightly colored sticky notes and cover your wall. Take up painting. Realize you are a terrible painter. Don't fret.

2. In the meantime, spend ridiculous amounts of money at hobby stores, music stores, or bookstores. Don't worry about it. Your thing will come. If the money worries you, make a budget. That's practical. Start it at the amount of money you would have spent on alcohol this week. That should get you started.

3.   For a while, consider dropping all "fun" things you did
     when you were drinking. When I drank, I loved to cook
     dinner. I use the term "cook" loosely because what I
     really loved was to drink and pretend I was Julia Child.
     Now, I thaw things and put them in the Crock-Pot
     around 10:00 a.m., and we eat them later. It's
     cool, dude.

4.   Allow for introspection but in limited doses. Journal.
     Pray. Go on walks every day. Get sunshine and get real
     with yourself. But do this for an hour and then move on.
     Let's be honest, as we hear at meetings frequently,
     "Your head is like a bad neighborhood. Don't go
     there alone."

5.   Don't treat yourself in a way that has a ton of
     expectations, money, or time attached to it. Take a spa
     vacation if you like, but realize, sometimes trips like this,
     when sober for less than a year or so, are not such a
     good idea. They can make you feel all, "This needs to
     be *fun*," which usually translates to "Everything is awful."

6.   Yoga and knitting. I am not kidding. Both of these
     activities have just enough rhythm and relaxation that
     doing them makes my brain sort of hum. Also, I can
     take my knitting to meetings, and then if I get bored
     or irritated, I just knit myself into peace. Don't try to
     do a downward dog during meetings—that might be a
     bit weird.

7.   Every morning, go ahead and ask your Higher Power,
     "Please show me something that will make my heart
     sing." I used to ask for Him to send me redbirds. They
     show up for me in the rarest moments. This world has
     wonderment and power. Allow it to heal you and
     inspire you.

8. Get a puppy. Go to the pound and save a little scared creature's life. They'll thank you for it.

9. Get a cat. Maybe you'll get one of Steve's relatives. Highly possible. You'll thank me for it.

10. If you're not a furry animal kind of person, get a fish. Or a plant? Get something to nurture. You'll be surprised how much it will nurture you right back.

CHAPTER 20

I Find Out I Am Not Hot

There was a point in my life when I could enter a room at a party, and it felt like the people in the room would stop and look right back at me. I loved it. But recently I realized it's a tiny bit possible that alcohol made me *feel* like they were looking at me, when really there might have just been a big clock over my head.

Currently, I am wearing my husband's wool socks, my yoga pants, and a large stained hoodie that endows me with the shapeliness of a matronly kangaroo. I am also wearing a stocking cap and some granny glasses I bought once because I thought they were funky—now I look two feathers shy of cuckoo. It's 5:12 a.m. on a cold morning. I am shuffling about, trying to locate my coffee cup and journal, and that's when it happens: I catch my reflection in the mirror. "Good lord," I jump. "There's a homeless person in here."

Nope. Just me. I am now a woman who has traded in all sense of cuteness and whimsy for a stocking cap and practical shoes.

I used to wear strappy shoes. The kind with heels that sent shooting pains up my calves, a nice reminder that I was being sexy. Sexy comes at a price, but not always at the expense of your calves.

I remember parties in my late twenties. It was the era of dark lipstick and long hair, and I would be dressed in red velvet and wear a lot of eyeliner. I weighed about twenty pounds less than I should. I am dripping with slouchy sophistication, my own little Dana Primetime Show.

But in my mind? I am sitting in the corner wearing a hideous Christmas sweater with a badly placed glowing reindeer nose and tinsel. Note that this is before the hipster irony of the ugly Christmas sweater becoming a "thing." I feel out of place and nervous, and all this, of course, leads to heavy leaning on a nice merlot that nicely matches my shirt.

What I did to deal with the constant questioning and agitation in my head was to carry around with me, at all times, an imaginary press kit and camera crew that filmed my every move. I would strut through the crowd at the party, talking and laughing and holding my glass, all the while with a narrator, usually one with a slick BBC accent, voicing over the proceedings like I were in an episode of *Lifestyles of the Rich and Anxious*.

"And now, our heroine tries to maneuver a beer into her cup from the keg, without looking stupid, because she has never really understood that whole pump thing and usually asks some boy to get her one. She makes light banter with the people around her. Inside, she is feeling like a clumsy fool, but to all who watch her spray beer on her shoes, she seems completely relaxed. She is now moving on to wine, which involves corkscrews, and for some reason tonight her hands are clumsy extensions of her incapacitated brain. She takes up her clever barrage to level three and is so charming most people swoon as she walks by. She is exhausted after ten minutes. Clearly, brown liquor is necessary now."

My narrator had no sense of boundaries. He would follow me into the bedroom with my boyfriend. There I'd find myself needy and seductive, a lovely mix of deep longing for connection paired with a grim determination to be interesting. This one-two punch was confusing to all involved. I wanted, at any cost, to be the cool girl who needed no one, who was so utterly fabulous that everyone needed *her*.

It never worked out that way.

To say I was a bit codependent is like saying North Dakota is chilly in January. I had so many unmet needs and desires that I figured would be fixed by romance, and romance answered back, quite calmly, "Girl, you nuts."

At a recent coffee meeting with a friend, we ended up on the bracing subject of our sordid pasts. My friend has been a follower of Jesus since she was three years old. She is adorable, clearheaded, and about as all together as a full set of fine china. This must be what happens to those of us who throw up our hands in surrender, at three years old, and wholeheartedly lisp, "I am Yours, dear Jesus." It is simply an easier path. Sure, when she described her last trip home for Thanksgiving, I breathed a sigh of relief because her family was about as lovably wacko as mine, but she is still a straight arrow. And she has the unbruised and trusting psyche to prove it. At any rate, when I described a few of my sordid-past interludes, she couldn't compete. I threw up my hands and surrendered at twenty-eight. You can do the math here, and my friend certainly could, too, but she was kind. "Girl, you love Jesus. He loves you. You just had to learn it a different way." True.

Now, marriage. And sex. And then, recovery. And it seemed I had to relearn sex, sober sex, because it was so much easier with copious layers of wine first. I had an addiction to alcohol, yes, but I also had an addiction to feelings. Big feelings. Sex had a lot of expectations attached to it, so much so that if my husband had any idea at all about all the expectations tagging along into our bedroom, he would have backed away slowly. I wanted security, romance, passion, nurturing, and constant attention. And that's just before eight o'clock in the morning. And I also wanted, at all costs, to be the *hot wife*.

Sex for me was all about lighting, special effects, and a bit of science fiction. I had no idea, really, how to just *be* in the bedroom. I had to be as CGI'd as possible. It was unnerving, all that posturing and animation. Most of the time my posing gymnastics, while a great abdominal workout, were just annoying. I had turned into the Jar Jar Binks of the bedroom.

How can one deal with sex when sex is so weighted down with expectation it can barely breathe? One drinks a lot, of course. And them, blammo! Sloppy and forgotten!

Sloppy and forgotten *anything* is no longer possible. When I first entered recovery, sex was the furthest thing from my mind for many weeks. Or months. Brian can tell you the exact amount. Everything was different, and for those first few months I was so raw and jumpy I fell into bed each night around eight o'clock. This was not a recipe for romance. I do believe there were a couple of teasing comments from Brian about "helping out with my tenseness," but I just stared at him with a sweet "touch me and you die" look. That usually put a damper on the whole nooky situation.

I didn't even know how to talk about sex with Brian. Here's what I really wanted to say:

"I am climbing the walls. I think if you touch me at any point anymore I will clench up like that poor girl in *The Exorcist* and start levitating off the bed. Don't take it personally, dear. But I never want to kiss you again. *Ever.*"

Putting it that way might have been hurtful. Instead, I said things like, "Oh . . . you are so cute, you little nuzzler, you. Here, I made cookies." Or "Wow, thanks for that great big hug that is lasting a really long time. Isn't there a Royals game on? Let's see!" Sports and food. They worked pretty much every time. I am in no way implying that my husband has the emotional depth of a Labrador Retriever. Somewhere in his sweet, blonde head he wondered what was up with the no nooky laws; but he is incredibly patient. And kind. And really into sports, so . . . thank God for that.

But, I missed him. And yes, I mean that every once in a while, I missed him in *that way*. It was fleeting, these random twinges I had for him, but they were there. And I knew, eventually, I was going to have to bite the bullet and attempt sober sex.

At one point, I decided the deed was on. I had on the appropriate stringy attire, underneath my flannel pajamas. I was wearing the scent Brian bought me on our honeymoon (the stuff he romantically calls our "sex perfume"). I had taken a nap earlier. I loaded up on carbs at dinner. I was ready. After the Thunderdome experience of putting the kids to bed was over, I even swigged a bit of coffee. I went into the bathroom and reapplied lipstick and more of my special perfume. As I moseyed back out into the living room, I noticed Brian's nose started twitching. He looked rather like a hopeful bunny as he figured it out, and I smiled at him as seductively as possible, because I was also trying to get a bit of laundry folding in prior. I like to multi-task.

It was awful. Just awful. I believe there was crying (my part) and some "It's okays" and patting (Brian's part). It was so epically bad I felt guilty for wasting the expensive perfume on it.

It was expectations all over again. But this time, I was aware of them. And aware of a lot of other things, too, like:

The sound machine is too loud.

All my shoes need re-heeling.

The cat is staring at us in horror.

It's too hot.

Now it's too cold.

Maybe I should consider doing yoga.

Yoga is expensive.

We're going to end up in a van down by the river.

I can't do this.

Later, as I cried some more, I realized it's possible I put a lot of pressure on myself for stuff like this. And I responded to pressure with about the same reaction as a frightened bunny. So, you know, sex isn't so good with a frozen bunny, unless you're into that kind of thing.

I have learned a few things about how to deal with all this from my meetings. One was "Easy does it," which basically means there will be a day when bedroom antics will seem fine. Maybe even more than fine. Also, I had been taught that if something isn't working, do one thing different. Since I really didn't want to tackle "one different thing" in the bedroom just yet, I decided to do something else divergent from my normal routine; I decided to talk to Brian about it.

"I am so sorry!" I started out. It was a start. I was back in the bed, stringy items removed, large sweatshirt and lumpy jammies on. I cried. He hugged. We talked.

I needed to start thinking of sex as everything it wasn't. It wasn't power, control, a way to appease, or a way out of something else. For me, sex had never been just sex. With so many layers and labels attached to it, it was fraught with its own self-importance. And, as mislabeled items tend to do, it went missing. When I decided to "let go and let God" and just talk to my husband, two things happened. I felt a little bit better. And I got rid of half of my stringy, lacy things because I'd had them since our honeymoon, and some of them made me feel rather ridiculous.

I did a few other new things, too. I understood that my body deserved better caretaking. I had been regarding myself as frumpy, like one of those "before" moms that goes on Oprah for a makeover. I was there. I had the hair tied up, baggy pants, comfort is my new love language kind of thing going on. I don't think Brian really much cared. As he told me once when I mentioned that gravity is a bitch when you get over forty, "As long as you let me see the parts I like every once in a while, I don't care about gravity at all." Brian could care less about wrinkles and gray hairs. He didn't notice that I wore the same pair of jeans for three days in a row. He was interested in the stuff stuffed in the jeans, I guess.

But, *I* cared. I cared about the sad woman I faced in the mirror each morning. I found that I cared for her. And gosh darn it; I wanted her to get laid.

So slowly, as the days and weeks passed, I took up running in the mornings. I stopped eating jelly beans and Twizzlers for lunch (most of the time). I wore "big girl clothes" instead of yoga pants and hoodies every day. Occasionally, I even used lipstick. I did not touch the sex perfume, however. I found I rather didn't like it as it was musky and sweet and reminded me of rabbits, copulating. Not good.

When I chose recovery, I had to put sobriety, and me, *first*. It sounds selfish, and it is. It totally goes against the mom code. But it's a good selfish to insist that finally, *finally*, you are going to get well. And then recovery helped me see that I had put my health and appearance totally last on my list, way below Brian, the boys, our house, and my job. It was down there somewhere with cleaning out the crisper drawer. I slowly got out from under my blanket of ugly because I wanted to know that silly, pretty girl I used to be, all the while celebrating the older, wiser woman I had become.

Yes, we did try again. One morning he caught me making the bed and snuggled in for a kiss. I leaned against him and sighed. "I love you," I said. "But this," gesturing toward the perfectly smoothed sheets, "is a big, huge minefield."

"I am very brave," he said. And smiled.

One night, after a long day out in the yard, I had entered that weird fugue state of physical fatigue that brings on happiness. Brian was changing for a shower, and I thought, *Huh. He's kind of cute. I'd marry him.* Endearing, yes? And lo, in our rather grimy state, we tangled ourselves up in the sheets and giggled our way through some pretty good nooky. "Solid seven out of ten," I sighed. "Solid routine and great dismount, dear. You really stuck the landing." Brian, always happy with sports analogies, heartily agreed. And I found myself, with all my folds and flab, looking forward to further practice sessions.

TOP TEN WAYS TO GET A TEN IN BED WHEN IN RECOVERY

1. Stop wanting a ten, first of all. Progress not perfection.

2. In fact, start using a lot of slogans when it comes to sex. "First things first," and "Easy does it," for example, are great in the bedroom.

3. Um, sock puppets?

4. Expect weirdness. Maybe sex was always great, and now it's not. Or, maybe it was awful, and now you are thrilled beyond all measure. Or, maybe a bit of both, and you never really know what your lady parts are thinking. All of this is okay.

5. When it comes to saucy behavior, patience is a virtue. Patience and passion don't seem to make good bedfellows, but they do.

6. Try talking about it. If you can't talk to your spouse at first, practice on a small stuffed animal, or a toy dinosaur. Don't let your children witness this, however.

7. Consider breaking into *Frozen's* "Let it Go" right in the middle of the hot and heavy part.

8. Consider that your husband doesn't care much about wrinkles or extra flab brought on by ludicrous amounts of sugar due to no more booze. Consider that he loves you. Consider that trust is part of this.

9. God put you two together. He is as much a part of sex as he is all the other stuff. Talk to Him. He'll listen. Take His advice, like throwing out the red thong that bisects your bum and makes you itchy. Your HP is right when He tells you that flannel jammies actually come off a lot easier. Thank you, God.

10. A sense of humor is the sexiest lingerie. No strings attached.

PART THREE

The Now

"You were sick, but now you're well again,

and there's work to do."

Kurt Vonnegut

CHAPTER 21

The Big Tell, and Me

The days that start with a trip to the Super Time-Suck Center are the ones that really test my recovery. And for that reason, I have tried to switch from my huge, garish, cheapo big-box store, to a smaller and much more expensive version that offers a bit more peace. But still, grocery shopping at any level is challenging. It was challenging when I was drinking, too. Why? Children.

If it sounds like I blame my children for everything, I don't. I blame them for *some* things but definitely not all. Grocery shopping with children for me has the air of one of those *Amazing Race* episodes where they're in India, and they have twenty minutes to repaint the Taj Mahal. There's a similar time limit, and everyone is yelling in Hindi, and there's a lot of weird requests, like, "Mom! Wats DAT! Canna I have? Can I? Please???" when we're heading down the feminine products aisle.

I'd been in recovery for over a year. My one-year anniversary was celebrated with a meeting and a chip, and a lot of hugs. "You wanna go out to eat?" my husband asked. I considered it, and told him yes, but not at a fancy restaurant. Fancy restaurants usually meant fancy bars with fancy bottles all lined up at attention, and I still avoided that scene. Why go to a place that makes you take deep breaths and count the beer bottles on the table next to you? Also, I wanted to pig out.

"Let's go to Bogey's and eat burgers and onion rings. And a chocolate malt. Oh, and chili cheese fries. And maybe a sundae. With hot fudge *and* whipped cream." My eyes lit up with the prospect. If food was still my drug of choice those days, then hot fudge was basically mainlining. But I didn't care. I was "happy, joyous, and free," as they say in my meetings. Whipped cream was just the topping on the sundae.

A year had taught me what to avoid. But, against my better wishes, I was at the Super Time-Suck Center. And I was not happy, joyous, or free.

My new beloved little store didn't carry Ovaltine. I never considered Ovaltine such a hot commodity, but as I texted my husband about the situation, telling him they did have plenty of hot cocoa, this was his response:

"NOOOOO. OVALTINE, PLEASE? IT IS SO GOOOOOOD."

I imagined him in his office, stomping his foot and whining at his phone, which made me want to text back:

"THAT'S A TIMEOUT, MR."

Because I practiced serenity these days, and service, I took a deep breath and didn't respond at all. I had only Henry today, so the odds were in my favor in taking on the Super Time-

Suck Center, for one measly item, while maintaining my grip on tranquility, right?

Well, as the poster says, "If you love something, let it go." I pretty much had to let go of my tranquility as soon as we walked through the sliding doors of the store. I don't want to attack my local box store. It's just something about the general sense of despair from the clerks and all the processed food packaged in a way that makes my toddlers snarl with envy since all we seem to eat is kale. As I ventured deeper into the store, I experienced something that happened every so often in this new year of being sober:

I lost my damn mind and wanted to drink something on display that looked like a Zima.

Triggers happen. The best thing to do is be prepared for them. Get a plan, get an escape route, get a layaway of chocolate and seltzer, and get your Big Book handy. Sometimes, triggers happen with no warning whatsoever. That's why they're called triggers. They are the sniper fire from above. They take their shots, and you're all, "What? I hadn't planned for this!"

That's the deal. If you want freedom, you have to allow for the unexpected. True freedom means occasional chaos. And it can mean that you want to scream in a boxstore as your son whines about sugarcoated, pink and green wheat bombs. I had already broken the main rule of shopping with toddlers: don't *even* go down that cereal aisle. And if you end up in the candy section, peel out.

I got the stupid Ovaltine. I got in line. I waited silently and fumed. I fumed at how unfair it all was. How I couldn't drink anymore. How it would be so nice to come home and have a nice glass of something. How I had married a horrible man who was going to cause my relapse because of a powdered chocolate drink. How everything was just awful. I chewed on all of this with great fervor until I reached the front of the line. The token teenage lump of sullen clerk asked, with about as much inflection as air escaping a tire, "How are you today?" Then he sighed deeply, to gain strength, I guess, to push out, "Did you find everything all right?" He couldn't muster an uptick at the end. Questions are hard.

I stared at him.

"Hi! I'm just great. I'm an alcoholic. How are *you*?"

Well, that's what I *wanted* to say. I didn't. I just smiled and nodded. There was a liquor store right outside the Super Time-Suck Center—I used to go there after nearly every visit—and it had just occurred to me that it was still just standing there. Waiting for me. My fingers drummed on the counter.

"Uh. The tape is stuck. I'll, uh. Let me call for help." The register hiccupped and stopped working, and Sad Teenage Clerk fumbled weakly with a few buttons. He did a great job of shaking his very long bangs out of his face, like that cute singer from One Direction, so that he could actually see the keyboard, but this finesse did little to fix the register. Henry spotted some Bic Lighters and started mewling for one. I was sure the top of my head was going to fly off and hit one of those fluorescent lights.

I continued my imaginary conversation by grabbing him by his apron and snarling, "*Don't you know who I am?* I am a bloody *alcoholic*. If you don't get me out of this store right now, my relapse will be on *your* perfectly mussed head. THIS IS IMPORTANT."

When I finally left the store, I added the following to my "don't like" list: Brian, Henry, the weather, my coat that wouldn't zip up the right way, football, and the economy. Squirrels. Boy Bands.

You get the idea.

Henry trotted along with me, gripping my hand tightly, and chattered away. I stalked to the car, loaded up Henry who was busy extrapolating string theory and how Sponge Bob makes cereal now. He leaned up against me as I grimly buckled him in, and I leaned up against him. He was smiling. Somehow Henry had absolutely no clue that I was imploding. He has no idea, often, that I do that. It's kind of the way of a four-year-old, I guess, to be interested in only cereal and annoying cartoon characters. I kissed his cheek. It was so soft, and he smiled and leaned toward me. "Hi, mommah," he said. My son has eyelashes that are impossibly long. If he can maintain them, he will be in his own boy band, one day. Perish the thought. I patted his seatbelt and smiled.

"Hi, Henry. Let's go home. But first, let's go get a chocolate shake."

"With der sprinkles? I LOVE da sprinkles!"

"Of course."

Of course. Don't we all.

Know what I also don't like anymore? Drinking. Because, I'm an alcoholic. So I don't drink anymore. No matter what. I survived the big tell to my husband, my family, and my kids. Now I needed to come clean to myself.

This is where Henry's discussion of the space-time continuum comes in handy. Recovery can kick your butt because it is forever. However, it's also so incredibly simple because I only have to do it one day at a time. This sounds like I'm just throwing slogans around, but occasionally contemplating how long forever is can only be tackled with a strong handhold on this very instant.

Recovery is a lifestyle. Some people embrace snowboarding, yoga, or owning forty cats as a lifestyle. I can say recovery is mine. I was no longer slogging through the minute-by-minute challenge of not drinking today as I did in early recovery—thank goodness. But when sobriety got comfortable with me, I found myself balking with it from time to time. I had invited recovery to live with us, a beloved but sometimes really annoying houseguest, for the rest of my life. One day at a time. And, at times, I wanted to give it a serious side-eye. It ate all the ice cream and then left sticky containers in the sink. It didn't care much about recycling. It spoke in cheesy slogans. If it could get away with it, I'm pretty sure recovery would wear a bathrobe all day, watch a lot of Netflix, and not shave its legs. Annoying. But recovery helped me keep my eye on the big picture without losing my focus, or my mind.

And I still shave my legs, so there.

TOP TEN WAYS TO MOVE IN WITH RECOVERY

1. Stop contemplating forever. That's crazy. Get through the next twenty minutes.

2. Get really comfortable with this: "God, grant me the serenity to accept the things I cannot change. The courage to change the things I can. And the wisdom

to know the difference." Feel free to insert saucy language whenever.

3. Acceptance is not defeat. Repeat that. Acceptance is *not* defeat.

4. Acceptance means that crap days will trigger you, maybe, to want to guzzle something. This is not defeat. This just means you are triggered. You are not a terrible, horrible mess if you are triggered. You are just an alcoholic/addict.

5. If you are an alcoholic/addict, you must accept that some things in your life need tweaking. If you had diabetes, you wouldn't surround yourself with Reese's Pieces and Swedish Fish. This is called "Acting Like a Grown-up."

6. Acting Like a Grown-up, at times, really sucks. Have a plan for that, too. Keep a stash of your favorite Netflix shows, cheesy magazines, fuzzy jammies, and Candy Crush apps available for these times. Allow yourself to wallow. For an evening. Or an afternoon. If you find yourself wallowing for days on end, you might want to skip to the next item on the list.

7. If things aren't going well, and life seems to be wonky, and you're feeling off, change one thing. Just one thing. If you don't pray in the morning, try it. If you've never prayed on your knees, get a pillow and give it a shot. If you haven't tried a walk in the late afternoon when the sun is slanting but you are tired out and want to just give up, get out there. Sometimes that one thing is a gentle reboot.

8. If the two previous items on the list are not working, and you are still all out of sorts with your recovery, your life, your children, or all of it, get thee to a meeting. There, you can breathe. There, you have one hour of peace.

9. At these meetings, sometimes the last person you'd imagine, like annoying Ron—who is a huge flirt and doesn't understand social cues—will say something that hits you right in the solar plexus, causing your eyes to fill with tears, and you will remember it forever. Or, it might be a sucky meeting. If so, I am so sorry. They happen. Sometimes all of this is really hard. You can do hard things.

10. Remember this: recovery is a pain in the ass at times, and annoying, and redundant, and terribly hard. And, at times, you would really like to have a big fight with it, like they do on reality television with a lot of crying, swearing, and throwing things, and then kick recovery *out*. But, recovery is like Hugh Grant's annoying roommate in *Notting Hill*. He loves you. Booze doesn't care about you at all. Tomorrow morning, recovery will be all, "Hey! It's a new day! Here's some orange juice and some yoga, and I even cleaned the kitchen for you!" Sign the contract and let recovery move in for good. Please.

CHAPTER 22

How to Survive Being Happy

I am an alcoholic who does not love to party. Most people think of the alcoholic as the one slurring about with a toga and something rightfully called an "Alabama Slammer" in her hand. That was not me. I would have happily drank the slammer, mind you, but I never liked parties. Parties were full of people, and, as I've discovered over the years, I don't much like people.

Let me amend that. I do like people. I love some people very much, but they are now a select few that I have chosen or who have, for some crazy reason, chosen me. We are a tribe, me and my people. I trust them. Add to that mix a bunch of other people, loud music, and the words, "Costume contest!" and I want to cry.

Three months into recovery, I received a wedding invitation. It was addressed to Brian and me, and I knew without opening what it was, all big, looping calligraphy on the front of heavy, creamy paper. I wrinkled my nose and set it on the table for later. As the day wore on, I snapped at my boys. I snapped at the cat. I snapped at our garbage for being so full. I snapped at my reflection for being so tired. I was sour and out of sorts and felt utterly uncomfortable, like I was coming down with the flu. A hot, dizzy feeling of dread clustered around my head, and it only wanted to manifest itself in what some would call over-the-top bitchiness.

I passed by the mail, and the pretty envelope smiled at me, all coy. "Go ahead, lady," it purred. "You know you want to." I opened it.

It was an invitation to Brian's old college roommate's wedding. It said so, right there, in sloping cursive. There was a date and time, and it felt like a bomb just exploded in my living room.

I reacted all over the place. First, tears. Ryan was a dear buddy of Brian's; I had met him numerous times and found him charming and sweet. I was happy he was getting married, really. But, how *could* he do so *now*? How could he invite me to this colossal college frat-house reunion that would be this wedding? Ryan was to partying what a Kardashian is to over-dramatizing. How dare he invite us? Does he not know how hard this will be? Perhaps it's fortunate that Ryan did *not* know. Poor man, all he did was have the gall to invite me to witness marriage to his sweetheart.

I had now cycled on to anger and talking to myself, walking in a loop between our dining room and the kitchen, muttering and holding the invitation like it was evidence from a crime scene. I said, "I can't do weddings," as I stared at the paper. "I can't do weddings."

And that's when I realized. I can't do weddings. This means I am not normal. This means my life will be forever awkward and scary because weddings will be, I am sure, happening all over the place now. All our happy friends will start hooking up everywhere like romantic rabbits, and I would have to contend with all this wedding bliss. In that moment, in my kitchen, I hated everyone who ever fell in love. Love is stupid. It just means people want to celebrate it and then push drinks into your hands, practically forcing you to celebrate all that mushiness right along with them.

I don't like celebrations. I hate life. I cried a bit more and conceded I was the Grinch of Everything. I walked out onto our front porch and contemplated the most depressing thing ever: I wouldn't be able to toast my New Year. And Halloween? No big pitchers of margaritas there, either. I couldn't see it, a dry Halloween. It seemed like such a fool's errand, all this dressing up in kitty costumes, when there was no alcohol to make me feel comfortable with the tail and whiskers and the lack of dignity. Plus, Halloween had strangers coming to our door. As an alcoholic, I hate opening doors, answering phones, signing for packages, talking, and being responsible—basic interaction.

How was I supposed to do life if life included all these fun things? Fun things had to be garnished by wine. Otherwise, they were not fun things. And I would be so terribly *aware* that they s*hould* be fun, making me want to drink even more.

I would now have to do all sorts of events sober. Anniversaries without romantic champagne. Anniversaries were supposed to be romantic and fun. Also, the Super Bowl. How was I going to deal with the boredom, the cheering, and the horrible halftime shows? Also, anything to do with Christmas. Christmas means Bailey's and eggnog with a kick, and who really cares about the birth of baby Jesus when you can't drink mulled wine by the fire while listening to Josh Groban?

We don't have a fireplace. And I never much cared for mulled wine; hot wine added an unnecessary step to drinking it.

Thanksgiving. Thanksgiving meant traveling, which totally strung me out, so that meant martinis at my father-in-law's house because he is a normie and was happy to oblige. He even had those huge olives that are like a meal in themselves, so who needs dinner? I could eat a martini or maybe two, thank you.

What about when I land a book deal? How can I possibly not drink when that happens? Brace yourself for the irony: I got a book deal about not drinking and yes, for about five seconds, I still thought, *Yea! I am so happy! Must celebrate now! Wine!* I promptly smushed that thought with, *You crazy! Call your mother instead! Post a picture of a kitty dancing on Facebook! Eat a Snickers! You don't drink anymore, remember?*

That morning, in my kitchen, it seemed impossible to accept all this happiness that I was going to have to contend with over the years. *Forever,* I realized, grumpy and doomed, *Forever, people will have good things happen to them, and I'll be forced to play along. Happiness sucks.*

I set the invitation on the kitchen table with disgust, as if it were a specimen for testing. I dialed my sponsor, ready to leave a rambling, whiny message about the difficulties of being me. My Higher Power shut this down because my sponsor answered right away. She is so awesome; she senses when my own self-ness is trembling with neurotic overflow, like a forgotten bathtub, or Niagara Falls.

"How are you?" her voice is all cheery and competent. She could run for president, I am sure. My sponsor has been in recovery for more than twenty years. I cannot even comprehend this number. Once, when I tried to explain eternity to my toddlers, after a rousing discussion about heaven and hell, there was such consternation from them that I almost backtracked and ended it with, "Let's all watch some television! Eternity shmirnity!" But I plowed ahead, all spiritual and informative, and totally freaked them out.

"Forever?" whispered Charlie. "Like, FOREVER, forever?"

"Yep," I whispered back. "Uh, it'll be awesome." Neither of us looked convinced. This is how I feel about twenty years of recovery. And about all the birthday parties, and the fact that Christmas comes back *every* year, and all those taco nights. *How* can taco night occur without margaritas? They're *festive.* I can't do *festive.*

I didn't get to tell my sponsor any of this. Instead, she distracted me with, "When was the last time you went to a meeting?" She could hear, I think, the catch in my voice. I counted the days; I had missed my normal Monday night because of a sick kid. It had been a few days longer than normal. Meetings for me are like an automatic thermostat. They are programmed to keep me stable, even if my environment is a below-zero, ice-storm chaos.

"Dana. You don't have to go to the wedding. If you explain this to Brian, and he doesn't get it, you still don't have to go. You're not responsible for him getting it. You're just responsible for you."

"I don't want to make them mad. I know Brian will want me to go with him. They'll all ask about me. What if they ask about me, and Brian says, 'She's a lush and I hate her'?"

Silence.

"What? It could happen. What if they all talk about me, and they form a large circle and sit around talking about crazy Dana for hours, and Brian agrees with it all and doesn't come home?"

"Dana. It's a tiny bit possible they won't do that. Because, it's a wedding. They might be focused on other things."

True. And I did talk to Brian, and here's what he said, "I support you, totally. You gotta do what's best for you right now." And he paired that with a hug and a kiss and somehow I felt like I was watching a Hallmark movie with the perfect husband. Except Hallmark movies probably wouldn't feature an alcoholic or addict as their protagonist.

Halloween came and went. I spent a horrible amount on candy corn stringy lights and the good chocolate candy, not the lame Tootsie roll mix, for the kids. I picked out all the Reese's. I sat on the front porch and got really sad and uncomfortable. I missed my wine. The night had a tangy chill, and I remembered so fondly, waiting for the kids to come in all their finery, the warm glow of a glass of wine in me to help me celebrate.

So, I did what my sponsor always tells me: I thought it through. We all know the route that one glass would take for me. I wondered, too, why I always needed help to celebrate. Why not just . . . celebrate?

"I really would like a drink," I tell Brian in a robotic voice. It sounds so dumb to say out loud, that I speak woodenly, like I'm spitting it out. I know that if I get it out there, in the air above me, it will dissipate a bit.

He looks over at me and says, "Nah, you don't. That stuff'll kill you. Let's take 'em trick-or-treating. And then eat all their candy."

So we did. And my boys, dressed as Charlie Brown and Snoopy, were so adorable I thought I might faint. When Henry walked, his little tail wagged back and forth, and I just followed, taking pictures and sometimes not, because just watching and breathing and cheering them on was enough.

I can say, after some time sober, that Halloween is now just Halloween. And Christmas is just Christmas, only better, of course. It is richer and more alive, and I really do believe in Santa for these Christmases because my life has magic now.

But weddings? Still not a fan. Brian and I were recently invited to another college buddy's wedding. Evidently, Brian has a lot of college buddies who didn't get married in their twenties, like normal people do, but are all getting hitched in their late thirties. *Weirdos.* Anyhow, as I eye the invitation and then Brian, I took a deep breath, "I'll go. We'll go. But, there will be some things in place. And I might need an escape hatch. And you cannot leave. My. Side. And, let's take the boys. Nothing like watching a toddler dance the funky chicken to distract me. Deal?"

Brian blinked, not at all realizing that weddings were fraught with so much fine print. "Deal?" he answered. He has learned that many things in my life have way more layers to them than he ever thought possible. I'm hoping one day he will find this *really* hot.

The actual getting married part of the wedding was divine. The vows the bride and groom exchanged brought me to tears. As I sat there, Brian reached for my hand, and I just held on and thanked God for this moment to remember who we were some eight years ago. It was a good moment. And it was a moment that totally redeemed what happened next. As we walked in the door to the banquet hall, I instantly located the food buffet and then searched for a bar. I always do this sort of surveillance. I spotted a large food table but not a lot of food. At least a hundred cupcakes were stacked in sugary splendor, though, so that helped. And, no bar. Wait, no bar? Could we have lucked into a dry wedding? Praise Jesus!

That's when I saw them, the bottles of wine, both red and white, all opened and properly chilled, waiting for me at the tables. It was a wine buffet, only you didn't even have to walk to it. "Oh shit," I said, calmly.

Brian took my hand, and we headed for a table. As soon as we sat down, I counted the bottles and glasses and was able to estimate, to the ounce, how much everyone was drinking. This takes skills. It's one of the tricks of the trade. Instead of sitting down while chirping, "Hi! I'm Dana and I'm a recovering alcoholic, and this is really my idea of big, fat Hell! Nice to meet you!" I murmured my hellos and waited for my kids to be cute so we would be distracted. Come to find out, the table was full of teachers. The horror. Teachers can outdrink *anyone*.

I survived. I took the boys outside a few times to run around and play. I ate a dozen cupcakes. I drank a lot of sweet tea. My glucose levels were skyrocketing so much I was seeing double, but I was sober. "I wanna dance," I muttered tersely to Brian as some Frank Sinatra came on. Brian had to go running after Henry after his fourth cupcake, so no dancing. He returned with a sugar-crazed toddler just as "Brick House" echoed over the speakers so loudly I felt the bass in my lower intestines. Brian looked at me and raised his eyebrows. I sighed. "No . . . I do not want to dance to 'Brick House.' Our children are going to need enough therapy as it is."

Then, Dean Martin started crooning. "Dance, now, please?" I asked, as Deano's buttery voice continued. But Charlie needed the bathroom, and I was stuck waiting again.

Thumpy music came on, something about being at a club and some shaking up in here. This music was of a genre that made women want to shake their behinds a lot. A few of them seemed really into it, like they were back in their twenties and were really, really good at shaking. I realized, with all the blessed clarity of the *one* person in the room who wasn't drinking, that these women were terrible dancers and way too old to be grinding on their partners to "Single Ladies" but, hey, to each his or her own. My side of the reception and all that.

But, all I wanted was my moment. Just a *moment*. If I can't drink, I'm at least owed that one romantic moment to make this all worth it. I want that moment when I look around and see my family and feel such love and gratitude that we could be right back in that Hallmark movie.

After one more pre-diabetic cupcake and more tea, I sloshed outside with the boys for another run of the perimeter. We would be leaving soon, which was good, and all in all the whole deal had been tolerable. I sighed. Very quietly, I prayed, "I know I really don't need to ask, but I would just like to dance.

One time. To a song that doesn't involve grinding of anything. Please? This has been really hard."

At that moment, Etta James started up with her sultry sweet voice, and I knew it. This was my moment. We were a go! Except, I was outside with two squirrelly kids and my husband was nowhere to be seen. "Boys! *Inside*!" Something about my voice made them drop and run. I followed them inside, running with the furtive intensity of Jack Bauer in an episode of *24*. Brian was spotted, four meters at twelve o'clock.

"Brian. Romantic. *Now!*" I barked. I saw the mother of the bride flinch as I stalked past her and realized I might have been a little curt. I smiled sweetly. Then I took a deep breath, cuddled up close to the Old Spiced neck of my beloved, and closed my eyes. And here it was. My moment.

My moment lasted about twenty seconds. Henry came over and laid down on the dance floor next to us. Continuing to dance, even though I tried, seemed weird. He was exhausted and had nearly done himself in with the cupcakes. I looked up at Brian, and he answered my gaze, "You ready to get out of here?"

"Yes."

So, wedding receptions are still not my favorite thing. But other joyous events no longer send me into a state of paranoia and despair. Take last Thanksgiving. The whole family headed to watch a light show after our meal. We piled into the car and drove, blasting Christmas music and singing along. We watched the lights flash and pulse to Trans-Siberian Orchestra, and we were all entranced.

We visited this display every year. But this year, as I sat there and turned to watch my boys' eyes widen with the glory of it, I felt it. I felt celebration.

TOP TEN WAYS TO SURVIVE GOOD TIMES

1. Saying "No" is a complete sentence. If you don't want to go, and you feel it's not good for your recovery, say, "No." You might be different next year. But maybe, for this year, just say, "No."

2. When you are at a celebration, saying "No" is also a complete sentence. You can even decorate it a bit with a "No, thank you." If someone offers you a drink, you don't have to run away, pretend you don't speak English, offer a ten-minute explanation, burst into tears, or even lie. You can just say, "No. Thank you."

3. Actually, if you want to lie, go right ahead. I might be a Jesus freak and all, but in this case, lying is totally okay. Why? Jesus wants you sober. Here are some stand-in lies that have worked quite well; "I'm on antibiotics"; "I'm getting over a cold"; "I'm in training" (this usually requires follow-up); "I have to drive" . . . There are a lot of options. I prefer to look mysterious and say, "I'm on duty." This is fun because if they ask about your profession, you just smile, put you finger to your lips, and walk away.

4. As always, have a plan. Make sure you have an escape hatch. Bring your own car. Get into it whenever you like and slip away, all mysterious and free, into the night.

5. Communicate all of this, as clearly as possible, to your significant other. He or she might get it, or might not. It doesn't really matter. What matters is *you* made a plan, *you* voiced it, and now, *you* are sticking with it.

6. If you get stuck at a table with a bunch of drunk teachers who slur their wine breath all over you, don't worry at all about disappearing into the bathroom to text your fellow friends in recovery.

7. But really, if that's the summation of the party, go back to the fourth item on this list.

8. Don't panic. It's not always going to be this way.

9. Accept that making a plan, having a strategy, and going through a few extra steps for your sanity are your best party planners. If you were sick, blind, or had a wooden leg, you would have to plan ahead a little, too. Deal with it.

10. Then, there's always this option: pretend the holiday didn't happen and wait until next year. It's okay. Everything is okay. Alternatively, you can go batshit-crazy and distract yourself to smithereens by buying every holiday decoration you can find. Or some combination of both. Just don't drink. Go to meetings, and don't drink in between. Even on the holidays.

CHAPTER 23

Unwasted Grace

"Where you going tonight, mommah?" The blonde asks, plaintive as a baby panda. I explain, again, that it's meeting night. "Remember, honey, it helps me be a better mommy."

He considers this, and then adds, "Well, you should go, den."

I walk to the car with a very large cloud of guilt over my head. The cloud keeps up with the car and follows me into my meeting, plunking itself down on my head as I find a seat in one of the less squeaky chairs in the back. My meeting room is not one for ambiance. Plastic chairs, bad coffee in Styrofoam cups, and some fluorescent lighting—the same thing is going on all over the world in other church basements. Sometimes, I wish for a comfy couch and a couple of throw pillows here or there.

We start, and one of the members shares from his daily meditation. He places his glasses on his nose and slowly unfolds a scrap of paper on which are scrawled these words: "Feeling good about ourselves is a choice. So is feeling guilty. When guilt is legitimate, it acts as a warning light, signaling that we're off course. Then its purpose is finished." He then looks up over his glasses, at me, and I kind of want to get up and hug him, start sobbing, or say something dramatic like, "That *does* it! I am *never* coming back here again! Too many *feels!*" and slam the door on my way out the room. That last option doesn't make much sense, but whenever I get overloaded with the goodness of God, my first reaction tends to be completely off base. Good things are hard.

I opt for quietly dissolving into tears. No one, not even the poor soggy dude next to me, hands me a Kleenex. This is a rule. Someone once explained it to me. "If you start crying, and someone starts to reach and get you a Kleenex, it's like you think they want you to stop crying. And since we're kind of full up here with codependency and shit, we are often too willing to oblige. So, no Kleenex passing. Just cry."

And cry I did. I cried because I'd wasted so much time. I had babies with me, sweet, soft, chubby babies, with me, in my own house, and I messed it all up. I happened upon a video of Henry when he was just learning to sit up. He would laugh and laugh with chubby glee, and I laughed with him. But, I wondered, how long was I *there* with him? When did I start to drink too much? When did it go south? Why couldn't I have just been normal?

And how do I keep my kids sober? What if they end up just like me?

And all those hours spent wanting to be done with a certain stage of their lives, like teething, not sleeping well, or the baby lump part at the beginning. It seemed like I was always just biding time with them, waiting for them to grow up to the next thing. Why couldn't I have enjoyed it more?

Why did I waste so much time?

I got up and my chair squeaked so loudly I think they heard it in the parking lot. My friend Marlene was talking, and she kept right on going as I snotted over to the Kleenex box and swabbed at my face. I had worked up to the ugly cry of no return.

I cried for my husband, for worrying him, and for the stupid fights. I cried about that damn carrot cake because it would have tasted really good, and instead bits of it were still shellacking our cabinets. I cried because I never got just how much of a sense of humor he has and how much he loves me until now. It took eight years for me to get that.

I cried because even though my children were not ignored or abused, they were tolerated. I cried because, now, when I come in to their rooms in the middle of the night and cover them up, I think, "You are so beautiful. You and your long lashes and sleep. You are the most perfect thing. And you are my boys." And this was not what I felt back then.

Well, I may have felt it then. A little. But I don't really remember. All the drinking, the pain, and the anger of that time has washed over everything, even the good stuff, and I am so sad. I have been told that God helps moms "forget" the pain of childbirth, so we will go ahead and have another baby. I feel also, in some ways, that my forgetfulness of the past is a way to cope with guilt.

I cried because I can't remember. And I want to. I want to have that time back. My children are growing up, and I find time and all of its blessings seem to be flying past me like that tornado scene in *The Wizard of Oz*.

Time is not the enemy in recovery. Our milestones and healing may seem to take so very long (even twenty-four hours can seem interminable), but they are happening. However, as my children grow, I become increasingly aware of how tragic my numbed-out state was when they were babies; I remember so little of their baby days.

When it was my turn to speak, I stared at my hands in my lap. The men and women in the room waited patiently. They knew what was happening. They were watching a heart breaking. This happens in meetings from time to time.

"My son Charlie will be five soon. *Five*." A fat tear rested on the end of my nose, and I smeared it across my face. I am sure I was really looking *pretty* good at that point.

"Five years old means school. Everyone keeps saying how nice it will be to have him in school, and then I'll really have some time to myself." Sniffle. "It seems all I ever wanted was to have all this precious time to myself. But, that's not at all what life is supposed to be. And now, I am just so sorry. I wasted so much time looking for the next event, the next break. The next anything to keep me from feeling bad."

A couple of them nodded and smiled. They knew this feeling. We fling ourselves about, to ease the discomfort, not realizing that we are only bruising ourselves all the more.

"But, I wonder how I could have been so selfish. Why couldn't I have been a better mother? Why didn't I put their needs first? Why?" I could not look up.

And then Marlene broke a rule. In meetings, no one interrupts or answers until it's their turn, but as I sat there, crying into my hands, I heard her voice.

"Because you're an alcoholic, Dana. That's why."

It was all the answer I needed.

TOP TEN REASONS I'M A GRATEFUL ALCOHOLIC

1. The relationships I forged with friends in recovery have been some of the most real, most trustworthy, and most hilarious I've ever known. Old relationships have deepened, too. Or completely dropped off the face of the earth. Either way, it's okay.

2. If I don't want to do something because it might threaten my recovery, I'm now able to say "No, thanks," clearly and distinctly. A lot of times in my head I say, *Aw HELL no, person. As IF*, but I don't say that out loud. I know. Smart.

3. It has become clear to me now that I'm not in control of much of anything. This is a huge relief. Also, I am not most important. Both of these things are good to really know, deep down, all the time. I'm kind of the opposite of Stuart Smalley. I look in the mirror each day and say, "I'm second. I'm of service. And gosh darn it, I like me."

4. I learned also that sometimes not everyone will like me. This is not as horrifying and impossible as I once thought. Neither is it something I have to fix. Thank goodness, because otherwise with all this self-realization I'd also be extremely busy trying to make all people adore me.

5. When I attend a meeting, something lifts me up, and often, when I really pay attention, I feel the presence of God sitting with us in the room. Not always. But sometimes. And it's amazing.

6. I have learned how to get through tough days without losing my shit. This, in itself, is a miracle.

7. Laughter. I have a constant inner ABBA soundtrack playing in my mind. I am the queen of bad jokes. I am a goofball but not because others are watching. Most of this takes place when I'm making dinner with Steve the Cat as my only audience, and he's only there so I'll throw him some cheese. I'm so hilarious I think I should have my own reality television show. But then, most ideas like this end in me reviewing the fourth item on this list.

8. My marriage. We are for each other.

9. My faith.

10. My life.

CHAPTER 24

Street Dance and Beer on My Shoes

When I was about ten years old, my friend Tracy and I were hanging out at my house after dinner. Tracy was staying for a sleepover, I remember this because it was rare. My house was never the hangout, and I spent more time at Tracy's home than my own. Tracy's family was loud and there were a lot of them. There was a lot of running up and down stairs, and The Beatles' *White Album* was always on the record player. My house didn't truck with such shenanigans.

I also remember that night because I ended up sticking a needle through the bottom of my heel, a good half inch in. That's rather unforgettable.

When I first noticed this, I was rather surprised. I noticed because when I took a step I found something tugging at my bare foot on the shag carpet and, when I looked down, I saw half of a needle sticking out of it. *Huh*, I thought. *There's a needle in my foot, almost so far in it's really gross. I should pull it out.*

No. Actually, that's not what I thought at all. Instead, I totally lost my mind. I screamed and hopped around on my non-stabbed foot. My screaming was so high-pitched and enthusiastic that my mom showed up with a kitchen towel in her hands. I must point out that every memory of my mom is one where she has a dishtowel in her hands. I know this means something.

Anyhow.

My screaming escalated. My dad must not have been home because he would have shouted some sense into me with a "Cut that crap out!" and I would have proceeded to, you know, pull the needle out.

Then I decided I needed to move. For some reason, the presence of my mom and Tracy made me fearful. They were going to touch it. They would try to touch my impaled foot, and I damn well needed to get away. So I hopped and screamed, like a freaked-out kangaroo, all around the house. Tracy and my mom followed me a bit, mostly saying, "What's wrong? What is *wrong*? Dana, come *here*. Dana, you need to *calm down*."

These words fell on deaf ears. I was too busy having an epileptic seizure, now in the dining room, when I lost them. They gave up.

At that point, I realized I was hurting. *There's so much pain! I must find my friend. Why is she not helping me?* With chattering teeth, I lurched myself back to my bedroom. I had moved on to full-out keening, something I'd only seen in old movies.

Sad ones.

When I staggered into the room, Tracy looked at me, looked down at my foot, and said, "Dana. It's a needle." And then she reached down and pulled it out.

In the last Harry Potter movie, the name of which I can't remember because they are all sort of *Hallowed Chamber of Big Fat Secrets,* Harry just up and kills Voldemort at the end. Boom, it's all done. I remembered thinking, *That's IT? It was that easy? Couldn't we write another one where, you know, Voldemort has an alien mutant baby, and we are on a spaceship or something? Write in Sigourney Weaver?*

That's how I felt when Tracy had the nerve to pull out that needle.

I had kind of enjoyed the freak-out.

I realize now that's how I lived my life for almost forty-some years. Almost every day there was something that would send me, or at least my brain, into kangaroo mode, and off I would go. I would bounce around my house, or my head, until I could grasp onto something that would tranquilize it. Wine and scotch—sometimes tequila nicely tucked away in a margarita or two—was the best remedy for this. Eventually, vodka in a juice glass over ice did the job. Until, you know, it didn't.

Then, when I decided to pursue recovery, the kangaroo stayed. This is normal and necessary because that hopped-up animal is all I had known for a long time. It loved me.

But, I did learn how to put it on a leash.

I still want to set it free on some days and watch it sock my house to smithereens. Some days I still want to take a drink.

Honestly? I have a brief hit of "Wouldn't a drink be nice right now because (fill in the blank with whatever momentous or bad non-thing)?" nearly every day.

Every. Day.

Recovery is not going to turn me into a woman who doesn't want to take a drink again. I've accepted that. Some alcoholics and addicts say their cravings totally dissipated. I envy these people. I see them also as the types of people who can now eat only one square of chocolate from their Cadbury bar, then wrap it up in the foil, and put it back in the drawer.

The weirdos.

I still want to drink sometimes. And I'm grateful for that. When it happens, I'm forced to stop, breathe, slow down, and say a prayer. I focus on myself for a moment, then, I focus on others. I get outside. Get a hug. Get going. Get rid of the burden of self.

All of these things are little meditative moments that bring me closer to God. And that's why I got into recovery, really. To get my God back. To get *me* back.

Another thing I got back was a serious ability to boogie.

It's a warm summer night with crickets and the smell of cut grass. The sun has just set, and the sky is a deep periwinkle. Amidst all this, I am shouting at the bottom of the stairs.

"Boys. DOWNSTAIRS. NOW. We're going. MOVE, MOVE, MOVE!! You will rue the day if we are late, people! RUE! IT!"

My children usually respond to this shriek up the stairs with at least three reasons why they must keep playing. This time was different. Thundering feet, followed by a bit of a kerfuffle with some pants on backward, and we were out the door within minutes. This, all parents know, is pretty much up there with when Jesus walked on water.

The air has the sweet tang of heat, and I can hear the music from my front porch.

"Oh, listen!" I tell Brian. "They're playing my song!" I strut ahead to the beat of "Mustang Sally" while the boys tag each other, and Brian brings up the behind.

It's the night of the annual street dance in our town. The summer is nearly over; school is starting; and our little town wanted a way to celebrate being its charming self. I had avoided this dance for the past five years. The only time we attended was when Brian and I had first moved here. We had lived here a month, and one night, as we were enjoying a beer on the porch, I heard the strains of a saxophone. "What is that?" I asked.

"I dunno! Let's go find out!" And we did. We didn't have children then, so we left. Right then. Stop for a moment to wonder at that.

And lo, there was Main Street strewn with white lights, lawn chairs, and happy people. Brian and I danced, and I sang along to "Brown Eyed Girl," insisting, as always, that the Van guy wrote it for me. And I felt young and alive. This is what one or two beers did. Gave me a great big happy "I'm *alive*" feeling that trounced, it seemed, all other feelings. It trumped everything.

Until, of course, I ended up drinking vodka that I hid inside my boots in the bedroom closet.

I miss those two-beer days. I don't remember exactly when the one glass of wine ended, and the vodka boots stumbled in. It doesn't matter much, the timeline. But occasionally, the alcoholic in me likes to spout, "Just one glass of wine! Just *one*. You used to be able to do that, you know! Try again! If you fall off the bike, you get back on! Don't be a quitter!" and all that crap.

Oh, but one glass was never enough.

I was never enough. I needed embellishment. I needed softer edges and more hope to lift the sullen dread that sat, heavy, in my heart every day. I needed to be the best wife, mom, and teacher on the planet. But even when I had done great things, and jockeyed to the top of whatever competitive mountain I was eyeing at the time, I didn't feel content. That feeling of never having *enough* was a maddening itch I could never quite reach.

I still get itchy for a glass of numb, and at times I feel frustrated that it still sneaks up on me. But, I also know that constipation is majorly annoying, and I get that once in a while, too. Both are a pain in the ass.

Tonight, as we walk onto Main Street, "Mustang Sally" has just finished riding all over town, so I don't have to subject my boys to future therapy instigated by me grabbing Brian and heading for the dance floor. Instead, we hang back by the face painting and the cotton candy stations. I am a bit wary because the smell of beer is strong; its yeasty breath is so prevalent I wonder if this was a good idea. I had stayed away from this for my early recovery years because I wasn't ready to be out, amongst a crowd that would take me back to my younger days at the Jazzhouse in Lawrence, Kansas. I had figured this year it would be fun. I had thought maybe by now I could just have a good time.

I take a breath and looked over at Charlie, who is sitting as still as a stone for the girl who was painting his face. His brown eyes look up at her, completely entranced, and he is a picture.

God, grant me the serenity to accept the things I cannot change. Please. Please give me the courage to change the things I can, and please give me the wisdom to know the difference.

I walk over to the cotton candy. Sugar sounds like a good idea. And there's my friend, Ethan. He is one of us. And he gives me the special smile and nod that we do because, seriously, we kind of think we are in some sort of secret, super hero clique. We have secret signals. We have special powers. At least, Ethan does, for me. His smile is wide, and I proudly show off my sons, whose faces are painted like a Pinterest fail. I thank God for Ethan. I turn toward the music, and then, of course, "Dancing Queen" comes on.

"Oh, listen honey. They're playing my song."

We meander through the crowd, talking with friends. We buy a ridiculous amount of sugary stuff for the boys, and I steal some of it. They don't notice because their toddler brains are ablaze with music and cotton candy. "Brick House" thumps on. I turn to Brian. He nods toward the stage, "They're playing your song."

We can't get rid of the boys in time. They cling to us with that telepathic ability of knowing exactly when we want them to buzz off and run about and get into trouble, so we can get our groove on. I wasn't going to have my moment any time soon.

I find my solution. I grab one kid and shove the other toward Brian, and we head out there. I am sober and dizzy with joy as I whirl and sing along with my two small boys. There is beer on my shoes and the pungent smell of booze all around me, and I am getting down. I hear the question, "Are you sad? Are you sad that all you had to change was everything?"

Henry stomps on my foot in glee, and I pick him up.

I am not sad because the kisses I give him are not soured with wine.

I am not sad because I'm a terrible dancer; I'm doing it anyway. Because, you know, it's my song.

There will always be a million reasons a day to pick up a drink. The gas bill will come, and I'll wonder if I can afford organic grapes ever again. Brian will be late for dinner, and I will detect a tone from him when he explains this in his text. Or, maybe someone will get really sick, and the hard stuff will pile on. Maybe the cat will throw up in my bed. Again. Maybe the sun will shine, and I will get a book deal. A million little reasons, sidling up to me, every day, to drink up.

And really, there's only one reason *not* to.

Me.

I'm enough.

TOP SIXTEEN REASONS WE ARE
MOMMIES IN RECOVERY

These are collected thoughts from my friends who are part of my super secret club. We, of the super powers, capes, and secret handshakes, we cheer each other on. We remind each other, of the enoughs. I tried to stop at ten, but I simply couldn't.

1. Being able to giggle and talk at bedtime with my nine-year-old instead of passing out on the couch. —Julie C.

2. Being the mom I am destined to be, not the mom I'm told to be or the mom I think I should be. Just the mom that I am. No more, no less. It's so freeing. —Alexis M.

3. Being sober allows me to be fully present for the stressful moments and the precious moments. I am not a perfect mom, but I am present. Drinking wine every day put me in situations where my daughter's safety could be compromised and now, if she wakes up at 3:00 a.m. screaming with a fever or if she falls and is bleeding with a big booboo, I am a fully capable mom who can take care of her. I am grateful to have no regrets. It is still hard and messy some days, but I know I'm giving it my all. I am learning to be fun and silly in recovery. I love to be a great example to my daughter on how to live a beautiful life without a cocktail. —Kristin S.

4. I now know I'm being the best mom I'm able to be. I'm not perfect. But I'm sober, and no one can look at me and blame me for their stuff because I drank. I hold my head up high with confidence and know that I'm enough. —Tonya S.

5. It is possible to have kids in recovery. I can show my kids how to live positively, in service and in gratitude; tell them about healthy eating; and pray with them, sharing my spiritual life. I read to them daily and I'm interested in them—truly interested. If I were drunk, they most likely wouldn't even be with me. Day-to-day coping can be hard, but nothing—especially not kids—is worth drinking over. —Libby S.

6. Being able to really be there. Before, I may have been in the same room with my kids, but I was somewhere else mentally. Now when they look me in the eye, they can see me. And I see them. —Megan P.

7. I love snuggling with my eight-year-old son at night and taking time to read to him. I also find my twelve-year-old daughter seems to cuddle with me a lot more. Not stinking of wine is a likely reason. —Mo C.

8. Happiness is a by-product of living a good life. Recovery is freedom. —Moira C.

9. I listen to my daughter wholeheartedly. We both have healthier views of each other, our daily lives, and the world around us. —Angel R.

10. The best thing about recovery is that it gave me back myself, and now I can fully give myself to my family, while still having enough left over just for me! —Heather A.

11. God has given me a precious gift: my children. I thank Him from the bottom of my heart for them. I am a grateful alcoholic, for if I were not alcoholic and hadn't seen the error of my ways, I would be oblivious to the wonderful gifts of life God has given me; and there are many! —Fiona S.

12. I find I'm a much calmer mother. I'm not rushing my beautiful boys off to bed at the end of an evening so I can open that first bottle of wine. —Tamzin S.

13. Recovery has changed the course of my daughter's life. The feelings that come from having a parent who drinks are now non-existent. It's not that she won't feel anger, worry, fear, and sadness in her life—but she will never feel those because of my drinking. Sometimes I feel like her life story started over at six years old, and to be able to see that she is impacted by my recovery is the greatest gift. —Mary K.

14. Being present is the biggest one for me. No longer parenting from a place of shame, which says that nothing we do is enough because we suck as human beings. Letting go of fear, doubt, and insecurity about who our kids are as people and all of the family dynamics, thereby letting our kids be who they are meant to be. —Laurie P.

15. Being in the moment with my children, and realizing there is no expectation that I should be a certain way as a mom. Those expectations sent me into a deep spiral after I had children, and it took a while to get back to myself. Now when I need a break, I tell my kids exactly that. That's a million times better that secretly chugging wine in the kitchen to keep up the appearance that everything is under control. Also, that I never have to feel shame again. —Erin S.

16. Reflect and write your own thought.

_____

_____

_____

_____

_____

_____

_____

_____

_____

_____

Self-Assessment Quiz

This quiz is often utilized in twelve-step meetings to help assess your drinking or other drug use. It is not a medical diagnosis, but it is certainly honest. The first time I took it, I thought for sure it was wrong. Then, I took it again. I probably tried taking it about thirty times before I actually stopped messing with my answers.

DO YOU THINK YOU MIGHT HAVE A PROBLEM WITH ALCOHOL OR OTHER DRUGS?

Answer these short questions with "yes" or "no" to see if you might need help.

1. Do you use alcohol or other drugs to build self-confidence?

2. Do you ever drink or get high immediately after you have a problem at home, school, or work?

3. Have you ever missed work or school due to alcohol or other drugs?

4. Does it bother you if someone says that you use too much alcohol or other drugs?

5. Have you started hanging out with a heavy-drinking or drug-using crowd?

6. Are alcohol or other drugs affecting your reputation?

7. Do you feel guilty or bummed out after using alcohol or other drugs?

8. Do you feel more at ease on a date or social event when drinking or using other drugs?

9. Have you gotten into trouble at home, work, or school for using alcohol or other drugs?

10. Do you borrow money or "do without" other things to buy alcohol or other drugs?

11. Do you feel a sense of power when you use alcohol or other drugs?

12. Have you lost friends since you started using alcohol or other drugs?

13. Do your friends use less alcohol or other drugs than you do?

14. Do you drink or use other drugs until your supply is gone?

15. Do you ever wake up and wonder what happened the night before?

16. Have you ever been arrested or hospitalized due to using alcohol or other drugs?

17. Do you "turn off" or avoid studies or lectures about using alcohol or other drugs?

18. Have you ever tried to quit or to cut back using alcohol or other drugs?

19. Has there ever been someone in your family with a drinking or other drug problem?

20. Could you have a problem with alcohol or other drugs?

If you answered "yes" to three of the questions, you may be at risk for developing alcoholism and/or dependence on other drugs.

If you answered "yes" to five of the questions, it is recommended you seek help immediately.

This quiz was adapted from a test offered by the National Council on Alcoholism and Drug Dependence. It is not meant to be used to diagnose a dependence on alcohol or other drugs. Its purpose is for identification of a potential problem. Only a physician or professional clinician should offer an official diagnosis.

Resources

National Organizations

Alcoholics Anonymous

WEBSITE: www.aa.org

Select your state to find the number of your state's general service office.

PHONE: A.A. World Services (212) 870-3400

Narcotics Anonymous

WEBSITE: www.na.org

Click the Find a Meeting button to find a meeting in your area.

PHONE: NA World Service (818) 773-9999

National Council on Alcoholism and Drug Dependence, Inc. (NCADD)

WEBSITE: www.ncadd.org

Click the Affiliate Network link and enter your zip code to find an affiliate near you.

PHONE: 1-800-NCA-CALL (1-800-622-2255)

My Favorite Sober Blogs and Online Groups

Stephanie Wilder-Taylor and The Booze-Free Brigade

https://groups.yahoo.com/neo/groups/Booze_free_brigade/info

I found Stefanie Wilder-Taylor through her book, *Sippy Cups Are Not for Chardonnay*. Stefanie is wildly funny and also, it turns out, one of us. We both had the same wake up call, but her call was earlier than mine. Imagine my surprise when I noticed her blog had started up a page called "Don't get drunk on Fridays." It was life changing for me to see her switch from "Yea! A playdate with tequila!" to a sober mom. Stefanie created a yahoo group called "The Booze-Free Brigade." It saved my life. And, she is still funny. Even without booze. Mind. Blown.

Crying Out Now: Voices of Addiction and Recovery

www.cryingoutnow.com

Ellie, the founder of this site, states: *Crying Out Now is a community of women speaking about addiction and recovery—*

telling our truths, and breaking down the walls of stigma and denial surrounding addiction—One Story at a Time.

Whenever I read these stories, I swear, I heard my own voice in all of them. It is powerful and real. And the women who moderate it are awesome.

She Recovers: We Are Strong and Courageous Women. And We Do Recover

www.sherecovers.co

Dawn's website is a candy store of resources, books to read, mentors to learn from, blog posts, and retreats to attend, all with recovery for women as the guide. And, she is funny. This seems to be very important to me.

Momsieblog

www.momsieblog.com

Of course, you can always go to my blog. At Momsie, I do talk a lot about other things than recovery. Like when I posted about how I couldn't find my phone because I was talking on it. Pulitzer Prize-worthy stuff.